As one of the world's longest established and best-known travel brands, Thomas Cook are the experts in travel.

For more than 135 years our guidebooks have unlocked the secrets of destinations around the world, sharing with travellers a wealth of experience and a passion for travel.

Rely on Thomas Cook as your travelling companion on your next trip and benefit from our unique heritage.

Thomas Cook **pocket** guides

FUERTEVENTURA

Jill Benjamin

Thomas Cook

Written by Jill Benjamin, updated by Barbara Rogers

Published by Thomas Cook Publishing
A division of Thomas Cook Tour Operations Limited
Company registration no. 3772199 England
The Thomas Cook Business Park, Unit 9, Coningsby Road,
Peterborough PE3 8SB, United Kingdom
Email: books@thomascook.com, Tel: +44 (0) 1733 416477
www.thomascookpublishing.com

Produced by Cambridge Publishing Management Limited
Burr Elm Court, Main Street, Caldecote CB23 7NU
www.cambridgepm.co.uk

ISBN: 978-1-84848-537-2

© 2006, 2008, 2010 Thomas Cook Publishing
This fourth edition © 2012
Text © Thomas Cook Publishing
Maps © Thomas Cook Publishing/PCGraphics (UK) Limited

Series Editor: Karen Beaulah
Production/DTP: Steven Collins

Printed and bound in Spain by GraphyCems

Cover photography © Photolibrary.com

CONTENTS

WHAT'S IN YOUR GUIDEBOOK?

Independent authors Impartial, up-to-date information from our travel experts who meticulously source local knowledge.

Experience Thomas Cook's 165 years in the travel industry and guidebook publishing enriches every word with expertise you can trust.

Travel know-how Thomas Cook has thousands of staff working around the globe, all living and breathing travel.

Editors Travel-publishing professionals, pulling everything together to craft a perfect blend of words, pictures, maps and design.

You, the traveller We deliver a practical, no-nonsense approach to information, geared to how you really use it.

The church at Betancuria

INTRODUCTION
Getting to know Fuerteventura

Fuerteventura

| 0 | 8 km |
| 0 | 5 miles |

○ —— City
○ —— Large Town
○ —— Small Town
═══ —— Motorway
━━━ —— Main Road
─── —— Minor Road
✈ ……… Airport

N

Atlantic Ocean

Agua Verde

Ajuy

To

Pájara

Cardón

La Pared

Granillo

Peninsula de Jandía

123

Tarajale

2

La Lajit

Costa Calma

Punta Pesebre

El Islote

EL JABLE

Montaña Blanca

Playa de Sutavent

Cofete

Pico de la Zarza

807

402

Punta de Jandía

2

Morro Jable

Jandía Playa

Punta del Matorral

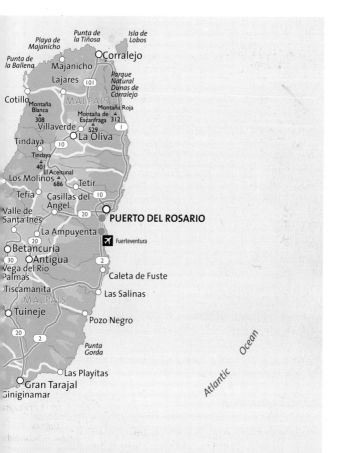

Playa de Majanicho
Punta de la Tiñosa
Isla de Lobos
Punta de la Ballena
○ Corralejo
Majanicho
Lajares 101
Parque Natural Dunas de Corraleo
MALPAIS
Montaña Roja
Montaña de Escanfraga 312
Cotillo
Montaña Blanca
308
1
○ La Oliva
Villaverde 529
Tindaya 10
Tindaya
401
El Acetunal
Los Molinos ▲ 686 ○ Tetir
Tefía ○ Casillas del Ángel 10
Valle de Santa Inés 20
○ **PUERTO DEL ROSARIO**
○ La Ampuyenta ✈ Fuerteventura
20
○ Betancuria
30 ○ Antigua 2
Vega del Río Palmas
○ Caleta de Fuste
Tiscamanita
MALPAIS
○ Las Salinas
○ Tuineje
20 2
Pozo Negro
Punta Gorda
○ Las Playitas
○ Gran Tarajal
Giniginamar

Atlantic Ocean

Getting to know Fuerteventura

Fuerteventura is the second largest of the seven main Canary Islands, with a distance of about 100 km (60 miles) between Punta de la Tiñosa in the north and Punta de Jandía in the south. Despite this, it is comparatively sparsely populated, with around 80,000 inhabitants.

It is generally said to be the oldest of the Canaries, mostly of basaltic origin, and as with all the other islands it has a unique landscape not found anywhere else in Europe. There is sunshine all the year round and a sea temperature of between 17°C and 25°C (63°F and 77°F). This island has very little rainfall and the water is supplied by coastal desalination plants. Fuerteventura lies 100 km (60 miles) from the coast of northwest Africa, and is between 30 and 40 minutes by car/passenger ferry from the neighbouring island of Lanzarote.

HISTORY

It is thought that the Majos were the original inhabitants of the island, believed to have come from North Africa. The people of the island are known as Majoreros (MahorAlRos); this word literally means 'people of goatskin shoes'!

In 1402 the island was conquered by Jean de Béthencourt and Gadifer de la Salle for the crown of Spain. The present village of Betancuria was founded by them, and it was the first capital of the island until 1834. Today's capital is Puerto del Rosario, which in recent years has become like a city-museum, with sculptures in almost every corner.

ISLAND DEVELOPMENT

The big attractions of Fuerteventura are the year-round sunshine, the wonderful beaches, the spaciousness and the relaxing atmosphere. Tourism did not really develop until the 1970s, when people discovered the beauty of this desert-like island with its white sandy beaches, golden dunes and the terracotta of the volcanic mountains. Add to these the lush green oases tucked between the hills and the astonishing turquoise seas, and you begin to get the picture. International recognition of the

GUIDED TOURS
See the sights of Fuerteventura with an experienced guide who knows the island well and can add fascinating perspectives on its history, culture and natural environment. Each resort has opportunities for guided explorations by boat, bike, horse or quad bike, which are listed under *Things to do* (W www.fuerte ventura.com). For a reliable and well-informed English-speaking guide who can take you to – and interpret – the island's historical and other sights, book ahead with Andreas Caliman (T 686 088 493 E info@fuertescout.com W www.fuertescout.com).

value of this environment was sealed in 2009 when Fuerteventura was declared a UNESCO Biosphere Reserve.

The island government (El Cabildo) was formed in 1912, and in 1927 the seven main islands were separated into two provinces. Fuerteventura and Lanzarote are administered by Gran Canaria, while La Gomera, El Hierro and La Palma are under the wing of Tenerife. The whole group is under overall control of mainland Spain, which islanders refer to as 'the peninsula'. A couple of attempts have been made for total autonomy, but these were refused by the Spanish government on the grounds that the islands are not yet economically strong enough. There was indeed a time when the islands of Fuerteventura and Lanzarote were poor due to lack of rainfall, but things are now very different with the advent of tourism.

Do not be surprised to come across hundreds of goats miraculously finding sustenance from the barren land. Goat's cheese is the second-largest sector of the economy on the island, tourism being the first.

You may wonder why there are so many ruined *fincas* (farms) across the island landscape. The reason for this is that Spanish law stated that, when parents died, all property reverted to their children. Problems arose when family members who had left the island could not be traced, either perishing on the journey or just simply vanishing; to dispose of a property, all siblings have to agree to the sale.

THE BEST OF FUERTEVENTURA

With its unusual landscape and year-round sunshine, your stay on Fuerteventura can be as relaxing or activity-packed as you like.

TOP 10 ATTRACTIONS

- **Watersports** No trip to this island would be complete without sampling at least one of the multitude of water-based activities on offer (see pages 17–20, 33–5, 37–8, 43, 45, 47, 51–2 & 73).

- **El Tostón** A stunning fortified tower overlooking the harbour (see pages 25 & 27).

- **Parque Natural de Las Dunas (Dunes National Park)** Europe's very own Sahara (see pages 16–17).

- **Ecomuseo de la Alcogida** Explore the islanders' old way of living at these reconstructed houses in Tefía (see pages 56–7).

◆ *Morro Jable, seen from the air*

- **La Lajita Oasis Park** Lush gardens are the venue for this lovely, well-kept zoo with plenty of entertainment and a huge herd of camels (see pages 73, 94 & 96).

- **Jandía Peninsula** Mountains, a nature reserve, plateaus, plains and stunning beaches ... what more do you want?! (see pages 77–8).

- **Vega del Río Palmas (Valley of Palms)** Check out the island's long-kept secret (see pages 64 & 66).

- **Pájara** Discover one of the most beautiful towns on the island and its unusual church with Aztec-style entrance (see page 62).

- **Isla de Lobos** A beautiful island nature reserve off Corralejo, full of plants and birdlife (see page 79).

- **Centro de Interpretación Los Molinos** Find out all about windmills and their history on this island at the excellent windmill centre at Tiscamanita (see page 68).

SYMBOLS KEY

The following symbols are used throughout this book:

ⓐ address   **ⓣ** telephone   **ⓕ** fax   **ⓦ** website address   **ⓔ** email
ⓛ opening times   **ⓘ** important

The following symbols are used on the maps:

𝒊	information office	■	point of interest
✉	post office	◯	city
▣	shopping	O	large town
✈	airport	○	small town
♨	police station	⚌	motorway
▤	bus station	▬	main road
✝	church		minor road
❶	numbers denote featured cafés, restaurants & evening venues		

> ### RESTAURANT CATEGORIES
> The symbol after the name of each restaurant listed in this guide
> indicates the price of a typical two-course meal without drinks for
> one person.
> **£** up to €15   **££** €15–45   **£££** over €45

◗ *Pale golden sands at Costa Calma*

RESORTS
Places under the sun

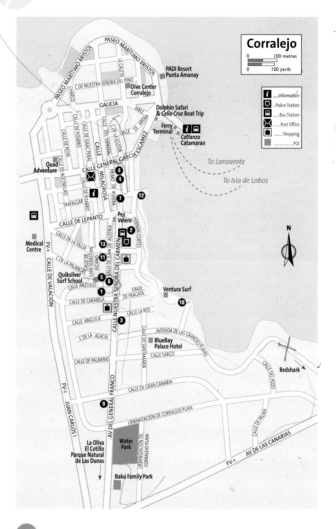

Corralejo

Corralejo is one of the busiest of Fuerteventura's old resorts, situated in the north of the island, with beautiful beaches and good facilities.

Like many of the island's resorts, Corralejo started life as a small, tranquil fishing village, with views from the little harbour across the sea to Lanzarote, the neighbouring island to the north. Having been hurled into the 21st century, it has become a busy, bustling town engulfed by tourism. Houses of many colours seem to spring up like mushrooms overnight. The nice thing is that each housing complex is totally different in design; they seem to be trying to outdo each other for individuality.

The main part of the town still has its old houses and winding alleyways, many of the former now converted to either restaurants or shops but still maintaining their character.

Around the old harbour there is an abundance of bars and eating places. To sit there with a drink in your hand, watching the world go by, is a delight.

The **ferry terminal** is also in this area, and there are little booths selling either scuba diving, fishing excursions, or trips in the glass-bottomed boat. You can book here for a trip to **Isla de Lobos** (see page 79), or a three-island tour, as well as the boat to **Lanzarote**. There is a café at the terminal, and there are toilet facilities as well.

Between the old harbour and the ferry terminal lies the **Tourist Office** (0034) 928 866 235, in front of which is a large, impressive statue by Paco Curbelo, a sculptor who lives on Lanzarote. Inside the office there are leaflets in several languages, telling you what is on offer for your entertainment, and the staff are very helpful.

The coastal road/dirt track to **El Cotillo** is not easy to find unless you know where to look. Opposite Corralejo's quay, and next to the bus station, there is a well-worn track that takes you on a beautiful coastal road trip, from which you see some of the best surf beaches on the island and the little fishing town of Majanicho.

You will find most shops are along Corralejo's main street (Calle Nuestra Señora del Carmen), although in the roads behind the main street lots of interesting places have opened, especially in Calle Anzuelo which is a jumble of bars and cafés. Side streets lead down to the sea, some to rocky shoreline, others to lovely golden sandy beaches. Here you can hire sunbeds, should you wish, and you will find eating places right on the sands.

If you continue along the main highway going in the direction of **La Oliva**, you will find on the left-hand side, just before the first big roundabout, a complex called **Baku**, which in the local Guanche language means a meeting point (Guanche is the name for the original inhabitants of the Canary Islands). A good place to spend the day, Baku is where Corralejo's markets are held.

Carry on further along the coast road signposted to Puerto del Rosario and you will come to the breathtaking **Parque Natural de Las Dunas**. This mini-Sahara lookalike is now a protected area. Be careful if you park your car off the road, as it is easy to get stuck in the

🔺 *White sand dunes at Corralejo*

shifting sands blown by the strong onshore winds. The local council has provided the main beaches with excellent parking areas marked by little wooden posts.

THINGS TO SEE & DO

Baku Family Park
One day really isn't enough to get round all that there is to offer in this unique family entertainment centre. You'll find eight computerised bowling alleys, billiard table, table football and other arcade-type amusements, all with bar, snack and toilet facilities. There is wheelchair access.

You will also find mini-golf, a driving range, a minipark for children, an aviary and reptile houses, a water park and an aquarium and seal show. There is also an Internet café, medical centre, municipal conference hall and theatre. All this is beautifully landscaped with free entry to the gardens and surroundings. Thoroughly recommended. ⓐ Going by car, leave Corralejo on the road to La Oliva; go round the first big roundabout and double back on your tracks. Baku will be on your right ⓣ 928 867 227 ⓦ www.bakufuerteventura.com ⓛ Daily. See website for specific hours of each section

Bike hire
Quad Adventure Quad expeditions are offered every day at 16.00 for about two hours. Quad safaris are every day at 10.30 for about four-and-a-half hours. Quad special tours (quad experience needed) can be arranged by agreement. Take your own picnic. ⓐ Calle Bocinegro 17 ⓣ 928 866 552/660 099 694 ⓦ www.quadadventure.net

Boat trips
Catlanza **Luxury Catamaran** Take a family trip on the 22-m (72-ft) *Catlanza* catamaran, which leaves from Corralejo harbour and anchors just off the idyllic beaches of Papagayo in Lanzarote. Watch for dolphins and whales on the way. Food and drinks are served on board (all in the price).

Those interested in sailing can help the captain and crew to trim sails and even take the helm. There is also the opportunity to have a jet-ski ride or snorkel (equipment available on board), or just to swim in the clear warm water.

Also on offer is the ***Catlanza* Exclusive Gold** for adults only (16 years and over). This excursion also sails to the beaches of Papagayo, but with a reduced number of guests and champagne cocktails served throughout the day. ❸ Leaves from Corralejo harbour ❶ 928 513 022 ❿ www.catlanza.com (make your reservation online and get a 10–15 per cent discount) ⏰ Trips 10.00–13.00, 13.30–16.30 Fri & Sun (13.20 in June, July, Aug)

Dolphin Safari *Siña Maria* Anchor off Isla de Lobos to snorkel, swim and enjoy a buffet with drinks (the price is all-inclusive). The same company also does deep-sea fishing trips. Beer and soft drinks are available on board. ❸ Kiosk on Corralejo Quay ❶ 928 536 105/628 102 617 ⏰ 6 trips a day 08.00–13.30 Mon–Sat, closed Sun

Glass-bottomed *Celia Cruz* Catamaran This boat has various trips ranging in length from 1 hour to 5 hours. ❶ 639 140 014

- a cruise directly to Isla de Lobos, where you can swim, departs at 10.00 and 12.00 daily (if you want to stay on Lobos for longer, you can wait until the last boat back, which leaves at 16.00)
- a mini cruise leaves at 13.00 daily (not Tues and Sat)
- a trip to Papagayo and Lobos leaves at 11.00 Tues and Sat (returning at 16.00)

For independent sailing or fishing excursions try **Sail Charter** ❶ 646 531 068/639 140 014 ❷ celiacruz@fuerteventura.net

Diving
Dive Center Corralejo The courses listed below include equipment, book, video, logbook and certificate. ❸ Calle de Nuestra Señora del Pino 22 ❶ 928 535 906 ❿ www.divecentercorralejo.com ❷ buceodcc@dive centercorralejo.com ⏰ 08.30–18.30 Mon–Sat, closed Sun

- **Discover scuba diving**: a short introductory course, with the option of an open-water dive at additional cost
- **Scuba diving**: a course resulting in a qualification to dive up to 12 m (39 ft) with an instructor. Consists of three hours of theory, three hours in the pool and two hours in the sea, over a period of three days
- **Open-water diving**: a longer course taking five days, with five hours of theory, five hours of pool practice and four hours in open water

PADI Resort Punta Amanay ⓐ Calle el Pulpo 2 (behind the harbour)
ⓣ 928 535 357/656 447 657/639 171 949 ⓦ www.punta-amanay.com
ⓔ info@punta-amanay.com
- **Beginners' course**: one hour of theory, one hour for a pool lesson and one open-water dive

⬤ *Take your pick from the many boat trips that depart from Corralejo harbour*

- **Open-water diver course**: five hours of theory, five hours of pool lessons, four open-water dives, certificate
- **Advanced and speciality (e.g. Nitrox) courses**: on request

Fishing

Pez Velero Trips for fishers and spectators. Bring your own food. Water, soft drinks, beer and wine are included in the price.
ⓐ Muelle Deportivo (the harbour) ❶ 928 866 173 ⓔ inge.sassen@web.de
🕑 Trips Mon–Sat from approximately 08.30–14.00, closed Sun

Surfing

There are numerous surfing kiosks and offices in and around the quay so only some are listed here.

Ventura Surf Offers a beginners' course of approximately eight hours. Lesson includes wetsuit and board. Also offers private lessons.
ⓐ Waikiki beach ❶ 928 866 295 Ⓦ www.ventura-surf.com 🕑 Daily

Quiksilver Surf School Professionally taught courses for all levels, including equipment, meals, lodging and transportation.
ⓐ Calle Anzuelo ❶ 928 867 307 Ⓦ www.quiksilver-surfschool.com
🕑 Mon–Sat, closed Sun

Redshark Kite and surf camps and courses, with separate camps for girls (*chicas*) only. ⓐ KiteCenter Caleta del Mar, Avenida de las Grandes Playas
❶ 928 867 548 Ⓦ www.redsharkfuerteventura.com 🕑 10.00–14.00, 16.30–20.00 Mon–Sat, closed Sun

---

FIESTAS
5 January Día de Reyes
16 July Nuestra Señora del Carmen

⬥ *Corralejo's picturesque bay*

Tennis

BlueBay Palace Hotel Tennis courts, rackets and ball hire are all available, plus a tennis coach if required. ⓐ Avenida de las Grandes Playas 12 ⓣ 928 536 050 ⓦ www.bluebayresorts.com ⓛ Daily

🔺 *Fun in the sun on Corralejo beach*

TAKING A BREAK

There is an abundance of eating houses in Corralejo, especially in **Calle de la Iglesia**, a street with atmosphere near to the harbour and the Tourist Office in the old part of town. Here you will find a variety of restaurants to choose from.

Citrus Bar £ ❶ Chill-out and fusion food. Variety of healthy and exotic options for breakfast, lunch and dinner. Wi-Fi available. ⓐ Calle Anzuelo 1 ❶ 928 535 499 ⏰ 09.00–24.00 Sun–Thur, 09.00–02.00 Fri (barbecue night), 09.00–02.00 Sat (DJ & sushi night)

El Patio £ ❷ Typical Canarian restaurant, located just off the seafront promenade. It's a long-standing, well-respected favourite, open since 1983, serving international cuisine. ⓐ Calle Hernán Cortés 16 ❶ 928 866 668 ⏰ 18.00–24.00 daily

Pizzeria Di Napoli £ ❸ A busy Italian restaurant serving generous portions. Wheelchair access. ⓐ Calle NS del Carmen ❶ 928 535 145 ⏰ 13.00–23.00 daily

Dovela ££ ❹ Creative Basque cuisine. ⓐ Calle de la Iglesia 21 ❶ 928 537 297 ⏰ 17.30–23.30 daily

La Mamma ££ ❺ Try the exquisite *nidos de verdura* (vegetable nests) or the black pasta at this chic Italian restaurant. ⓐ Calle Anzuelo 4 ❶ 928 537 438 ✉ lamammafuerteventura@hotmail.es ⏰ 08.00–24.00 daily

La Scarpetta ££ ❻ Home-made pasta, eco-dynamic wines and gorgeous desserts. ⓐ Calle de Juan de Austria ❶ 928 535 887/ 660 101 275 ⏰ 12.30–15.00, 18.00–23.00 Mon–Sat, closed Sun ❶ Reservations recommended

RESORTS

Taj Mahal ££ ❼ Children's menu, good Indian food and drinks. Parties catered for. Lunch and dinner takeaway. ⓐ Calle Almirante Nelson 3–5 ❶ 669 740 966 ❸ 18.00–24.00 daily

Tio Bernabe ££ ❽ Lovely Canarian food in Corralejo old town. Live Canarian music. ⓐ Calle de la Iglesia 9 ❶ 928 535 895 ❸ 12.00–24.00 daily

El Toro Bravo ££ ❾ Popular steak house using high-quality ingredients. ⓐ La Tafeña Local ❶ 928 531 751 ❸ 11.00–23.30 daily

Waikiki Bistro ££ ❿ Lunch with fantastic views right on Corralejo's town beach front. ⓐ Calle Aristides Hernández Morán 11 ❶ 928 535 647 ❸ 10.00–18.00 daily

Infusion Restaurante £££ ⓫ New to town and noted for its fresh ingredients and genial service. ⓐ Calle Crucero Baleares 21 ❶ 633 551 354 ❸ 12.00–23.00 daily

La Marquesina £££ ⓬ Excellent restaurant in the small harbour, serving fresh fish. Sama baked in a salt crust is one of their many delights. ⓐ Muelle Chico ❶ 928 535 435 ❸ 10.00–23.30 daily

AFTER DARK

Corralejo has the liveliest nightlife on Fuerteventura, but don't expect its variety to match the big resorts of Tenerife.

The Rock Island ⓭ Popular bar known for top-quality acoustic music, with different artists performing each night. ⓐ Calle Crucero Baleares 8 ❶ 928 535 346 ⓦ www.rockislandbar.com ❸ From 19.30 daily

Waikiki Latin Club ❿ This is where the beachfront action is at night, with live Latin music until the last surfer drops. ⓐ Calle Aristides Hernández Morán ❶ 928 535 647 ❸ From 18.00 daily

El Cotillo

Small, charmingly old-fashioned and good for bathing and surfing, El Cotillo is a place in which to chill out and is still a comparatively unspoilt seaside village. It has some wonderful seafood restaurants and offers excellent accommodation, such as the complex of studio apartments on the beach called Cotillo Sunset.

Around the old harbour the area is traditional, with little roads, somewhat reminiscent of those in Cornish towns, which lead down to the sea. Looking out to sea is a beautiful sculpture of a lady by Paco Curbelo, and another of two fishermen with a boat. On the quayside are two restaurants with indoor and outdoor seating. The atmosphere is peaceful, with gentle waves lapping over the rocks. The beach is very stony, but the local children seem oblivious to this and swim happily in the sheltered bay.

West of the village there is a huge sweep of beach next to the aquamarine sea, and windsurfers flit across the water like dragonflies. To the east are some beautiful lagoons surrounded by rock pools and good beaches. It's a safe area for children and adults to swim, as it is protected from the rough seas. Here you will find several unusual-looking houses. Originally built illegally, somehow they have survived and some are for holiday rental.

About 3 km (2 miles) out of the village, you will come across El Faro del Tostón (the lighthouse). The nearer you get to the lighthouse, the quieter the area becomes.

THINGS TO SEE & DO

El Tostón

A visit to this fortified tower on the cliffs overlooking the harbour is a must. In the 15th century Jean de Béthencourt built a castle on these grounds to protect the little port from invaders. This fell into disrepair and the present tower was begun in 1700. Three iron cannons once defended the coast, and the tower could accommodate a garrison of 12 men.

◆ *El Tostón stands above the rocky coastline at El Cotillo*

Nowadays the tower is a centre for history and culture for islanders and visitors alike, hosting art exhibitions in conjunction with the Tourist Office. The lighthouse, which has been recently renovated, has an interesting new fishing museum. El Cotillo was originally called El Tostón, but was renamed in the middle of the last century. ⓐ Paseo de Rico Roque ⓣ 928 207 967, 928 866 235 ⓛ 09.00–15.00 Mon–Fri, 09.00–14.00 Sat–Sun

Museo de la Pesca Tradicional (Museum of Traditional Fishing) Small, but with interesting displays and audiovisual presentations, the building at the base of the lighthouse explores traditional fishing on this wild coast. A small shop and a café overlooking the sea complete the complex. ⓐ Punta Ballena (coastal road north of El Cotillo) ⓣ 639 438 319 ⓛ 10.00–18.00 Tues–Sat

TAKING A BREAK

El Tostón Bar & Restaurant £ A British-owned bar and restaurant, visitors come from all over to eat here. It overlooks the old harbour of El Cotillo. ⓐ Calle Muelle Los Pescadores 2 ⓣ 928 538 489 ⓛ Food served daily from 09.30

El Chiringuito de Torino ££ This lovely beach hut on the first lagoon beach, run by a local fisherman and his English wife, serves one of the best paellas on the island. No phone. Book on your way to the beach to have your paella ready for lunchtime.

La Marisma ££ Fresh fish and Canarian food. ⓐ Calle Santos Tomás, near the French bakery ⓣ 928 538 543 ⓛ 12.00–23.00 daily

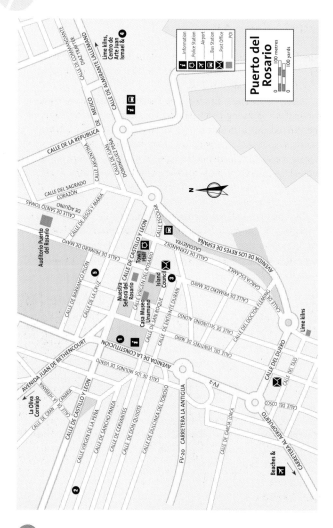

Puerto del Rosario

0 — 100 metres
0 — 100 yards

- ℹ️ Information
- 🚓 Police Station
- ✈️ Airport
- 🚌 Bus Station
- ✉️ Post Office
- ⬛ POI

Lime kilns, Centro de Arte Juan Ismael & ④

CALLE DE COMMANDANTE
CALLE DE DALTANTER
CALLE DE ALMIRANTE LALLEMAND
DE MÉXICO
CALLE DE LA REPÚBLICA
CALLE ARGENTINA
CALLE DE JUAN DOMÍNGUEZ PEÑA
CALLE DEL SAGRADO CORAZÓN
CALLE DE SANTO TOMÁS DE AQUINO
CALLE DE JESÚS Y MARÍA
CALLE DE PRIMERO DE MAYO
Auditorio Puerto del Rosario
CALLE DE CASTILLO Y LEON
CALLE ESCOLAR
Town Hall
CALLE DE FERNÁNDEZ CASTAÑEYRA
AVENIDA DE LOS REYES DE ESPAÑA
CALLE GARCÍA ESCÁMEZ
Nuestra Señora del Rosario
Island Council ③
Casa Museo Unamuno
CALLE VIRGEN DEL ROSARIO
CALLE DE BARRANCO PILÓN ⑤
CALLE DE LA CRUZ
CALLE DE PRIMERO DE MAYO
CALLE DE SAN ROQUE
CALLE DE ENTIENTE DUBÁN
CALLE DE SECUNDINO ALONSO
CALLE DEL DOCTOR FLEMING
CALLE DE NEWTON
Lime kilns
AVENIDA JUAN DE BETHENCOURT ①
AVENIDA DE LA CONSTITUCIÓN
CALLE DE LOS MOLINOS DE VIENTO
CALLE DE VEINTITRES DE MAYO
FV-2
La Oliva Corralejo
CALLE DE TENSA
CALLE DE GRAN CANARIA
CALLE DE CASTILLO Y LEÓN
CALLE VIRGEN DE LA PEÑA
CALLE DE SANCHO PANZA
CALLE DE CERVANTES
CALLE DE DON QUIJOTE
CALLE DE DULCINEA DEL TOBOSO
FV-20
CARRETERA LA ANTIGUA
CALLE DE GRACÍA LORCA
CALLE DEL COSCO
CALLE DEL DUERO
CALLE DEL TAJO
Beaches &
CARRETERA AL AEROPUERTO
② ②
N

Puerto del Rosario

Puerto del Rosario has been the capital of Fuerteventura since 1860. Previously called Puerto Cabras (Goat's Port), it was renamed in 1956 to sound more appealing to tourists.

Puerto del Rosario is an important business, cultural and recreational centre. It is a sprawling, developing place, constantly growing and being modernised, with a thriving cargo and passenger harbour, and is only 5 km (3 miles) from the airport. Part of the harbour has recently undergone a transformation, offering souvenir shops, cafés and bars. Around the oldest part of the harbour, you will pass through narrow alleyways and quiet side streets, glimpsing the tops of trees and bushes behind garden walls.

Between 1975 and 1995 Puerto del Rosario was home to the Spanish Foreign Legion, transferred from Africa when Spain withdrew from the Spanish Sahara. Puerto del Rosario is great for those who love shopping and art. There is also a large church with, oddly, a licensed bar in its grounds!

◆ *Puerto del Rosario*

THINGS TO SEE & DO

Auditorio Puerto del Rosario

Concerts and dances. Tickets can be bought during the two hours beforehand at the box office, or you can reserve by telephone.
🅐 Calle Ramiro de Maeztú 1 🕿 928 532 186 🕒 Events usually begin at 21.00

Casa Museo Unamuno

This was the hotel where the writer and philosopher Miguel de Unamuno lived in exile for some time, having spoken out about the dictatorship of Primo de Rivera in 1924. 🅐 Calle Virgen del Rosario 11 🕿 928 862 376 🕒 09.00–13.00, 17.00–19.00 Mon–Fri, 10.00–13.00 Sat, closed Sun

Centro de Arte Juan Ismael

An arts centre which holds exhibitions of varying types. 🅐 Calle Almirante Lallemand 30 🕿 928 859 750 🕒 10.00–13.00, 17.00–21.00 Tues–Sat, closed Sun & Mon

Lime kilns

Along the coastal strip and on some access routes to the town are the remains of lime kilns (*hornos de cal*), an industry lasting from the 17th century to the start of the 21st. Lime was exported to Gran Canaria, Tenerife and La Palma, and was used to paint houses and other buildings.

> ### FIESTAS
> **5 January** Los Tres Reyes
> **24 June** at El Matorral San Juan
> **29 June** at Guisguey San Pedro
> **4 August** at Tetir Santo Domingo de Guzman
> **7 October** Nuestra Señora del Rosario
> **30 November** at Tetir San Andrés

Sculptures
The modern-day capital is especially proud of its sculptures, on display throughout the town. You will find them in pedestrianised areas, on roundabouts, squares and streets, even on the shore near the harbour. Involvement in this project has led to the holding of the annual international sculpture symposium, where sculptors create their works in public.

TAKING A BREAK

Chino Gran Mundo £ ❶ Clean, cheap and reliable. ➂ Avenida de la Constitución 2 ☎ 928 859 304 🕑 11.30–16.30, 19.30–24.00 daily

Ristorante Julio Cesar £ ❷ Serves the best pizzas in town, also all types of Italian delights such as meat and fish carpaccio, and fresh pasta. ➂ Calle Virgen de la Peña 103 ☎ 928 858 252 🕑 13.00–16.00 Wed–Sat, 20.00–23.30 Tues–Sun, closed Mon

La Saranda £ ❸ This cute little place serves a variety of great tapas, freshly caught fish and a host of delicious seafood. ➂ Calle de Primero de Mayo 46 ☎ 928 530 330 🕑 08.00–17.00 Mon–Sat, closed Sun

Cangrejo Colorao ££ ❹ Overlooking the sea, this traditional restaurant has a menu in Spanish only, but helpful professional waiters will assist with any translations. The stuffed mussels are a speciality, but you can't go wrong with any choice here. ➂ Calle Juan Ramón Jiménez 1 ☎ 928 858 477 🕑 17.00–23.00 Tues–Sun, closed Mon

El Sitio £££ ❺ Chic upmarket establishment with a great cocktail selection. A paradise for gourmets. ➂ Calle de la Cruz 26 ☎ 928 532 012 🕑 Opening hours vary, phone to book

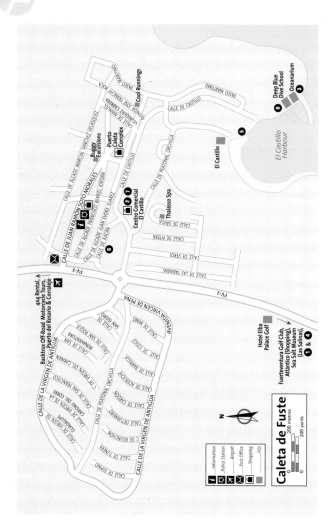

Caleta de Fuste

Legend:
- *i* Information
- Police Station
- Airport
- Post Office
- Shopping
- POI

Map labels:
- Cool Runnings
- Deep Blue Dive School
- Oceanarium
- AVENIDA JOSÉ FRANCHY ROCA
- PASEO MARITIMO
- CALLE DE CASTILLO
- El Castillo Harbour
- Puerto Caleta Complex
- Buggy Excursions
- CALLE DE CASTILLO
- CALLE DE JUAN RAMÓN SOTO MORALES
- CALLE DE ALCALDE MARCIAL SÁNCHEZ VELÁZQUEZ
- CALLE DE ALCALDE FRANCISCO BERRIEL JORDÁN
- CALLE DE ALCALDE JUAN FLORA SUÁREZ
- CALLE DE ANCÓN
- Centro Comercial El Castillo
- Thalasso Spa
- El Castillo
- CALLE DE PLAYONAL ORCHILLA
- CALLE DE SEVILLA
- CALLE DE PITERA
- CALLE DE VEROL
- CALLE DE LAS TARABIAS
- FV-2
- 4x4 Rental, Backtrax Off-Road, Motorcycle Tours, Puerto del Rosario & Corralejo
- FV-2
- AVENIDA VIRGEN DE PEÑA
- Hotel Elba Palace Golf
- Fuerteventura Golf Club, Atlántico (Shopping), Sea Salt Museum (Las Salinas),
- CALLE DE MIMO
- CALLE DE COSCO
- CALLE DE BARRILLA
- CALLE DE ACEBUCHE
- CALLE DE CARDÓN
- CALLE DE DETUNERO
- CALLE DE PLAYONAL ORCHILLA
- CALLE DE VERÓN
- CALLE DE RELINCHÓN
- CALLE DE LA VIRGEN DE ANTIGUA
- CALLE DE TUNERA
- CALLE DE ESPINO
- CALLE DE SAN ROQUE
- CALLE DE SAN ISIDRO
- BOMARENTUNA
- C. DE SAN FRANCISCO
- C. DE VIRGEN DEL CARMEN
- CALLE DE SAN FRANCISCO
- CANDAD DEL CONDE
- CALLE DE LA GUADALUPE
- CALLE DE VIRGEN DE
- CALLE DE LA VIRGEN DE ANTIGUA

Scale: 0 – 200 metres / 0 – 200 yards

N

Caleta de Fuste

This town is one of the main resorts. Located in the middle of the east coast, it is very convenient for the airport.

Caleta de Fuste is built around a horseshoe-shaped bay with a safe, sandy beach, so it is a good choice for holidaymakers with small children. You can surf (even as a beginner), dive, cycle, play tennis or squash, and take yachting trips with picnics or go deep-sea angling. Golf plays a big part in the district's entertainment.

El Castillo (the castle) was built in 1741 to defend the area from invaders, and shows how important Caleta de Fuste was in the 18th century. Today it stands next to a harbour complex with restaurants, bars, watersports facilities and a supermarket. There are also many bars and restaurants in the centre of town around El Castillo Commercial Centre.

To travel to **Puerto del Rosario** by bus, take the No 3, which leaves once an hour.

THINGS TO SEE & DO

Atlántico

This is a lively shopping and entertainment centre where you will find a six-screen cinema that shows Spanish-language films, 40 shops with some very recognisable names among them and a supermarket. There is a bowling centre with ten lanes, and many restaurants and snack bars. In addition, a bank is open all day, seven days a week. ⓐ Across from the golf course on the main road out of Caleta de Fuste, towards Jandía ⓛ The cinema, bowling alley and restaurants remain open well into the early hours

Boat-based activities

Oceanarium *Explorer* The *Explorer* is a glass-bottomed submarine, and the activity takes 90 minutes. A guide describes the most common fish found in local waters, including a type of shark and stingrays, most of which can be seen in the Oceanarium. Some you can even feed or touch.

● *Caleta de Fuste's picturesque harbour*

Finally, Harley the sea lion will emerge from the water with his sea lion pals and come on deck to greet the visitors. ❸ Puerto Deportivo El Castillo ❶ 928 163 514/630 758 648 Ⓦ www.oceanarium-explorer.com 🕒 Ring for details of excursion times

Oceanarium Catamaran In the summer season, after a visit to the Oceanarium, you can take an afternoon trip on the island's biggest catamaran, which will take you on a search for marine life. Throughout the year, dolphins and whales are seen on an average of 40 per cent of the trips. The marine turtles of Pozo Negro are seen most days. You get a chance to snorkel or swim in Pozo Negro with yet more marine species.

ⓐ Puerto Deportivo El Castillo ☎ 928 163 514/630 758 648 🕐 Ring for
details of excursion times

Golf

Fuerteventura Golf Club There is an 18-hole, par-70 golf course 4 km
(2½ miles) from Caleta de Fuste and 8 km (5 miles) from the airport.
Part of a 5-star hotel, it is also open to non-residents. It is predomi-
nantly flat except for the last two holes, and there are three lakes with a
stream meandering through the course. Buggy paths connect all holes.
It has a 50-bay driving range, large putting green and a second one
for chipping and bunker shots. Professional tuition is available in
various languages. Buggies, trolleys and two classes of clubs can
be hired. There is a large pro shop in the main foyer of the hotel.
ⓐ Carretera de Jandía, 11 km ☎ 928 160 034 🅦 www.fuerteventura
golfclub.com 🕐 08.00–20.00 daily

Hotel Elba Palace Golf This golf resort, with 5 stars, is set amidst a village
of quality houses of differing designs. The hotel-cum-clubhouse has
been built in the Canarian style of architecture, with beautiful
traditional balconies. There is an attractive inner patio with palm trees,
just the place to sit and relax after a strenuous round of golf. There are
61 en-suite bedrooms, all with air conditioning, minibar, satellite TV and
a safe. There is a gymnasium, floodlit artificial grass paddle/tennis court,
swimming pool for adults and a separate children's pool. The mature
gardens are an excellent place in which to take a stroll away from the
heat of the sun. ☎ 928 163 922/+44 (0) 871 423 5051 🖷 928 163 923
🅦 www.hoteleselba.com 🕐 Golf course 08.00–20.00 daily

Health and beauty

Thalasso Spa Fuerteventura Located in the Barceló Hotel on the edge of
the beach in Caleta de Fuste, this wellness centre offers a huge variety of
health and beauty treatments, such as mud wrapping, massage, facials,
thalassotherapy, waxing and hair removal. There are six pools, both
indoor and outdoor, a geyser, bubble beds, water jets and whirlpool.

Specific body treatments include Aquagym™ and stretching (for over 15-year-olds). Manicures, pedicures, eyebrow and eyelash tinting and a three-day anti-stress course are also available. ❸ Barceló Fuerteventura Thalasso Spa, Calle de Sávila ❶ 928 547 517 Ⓦ www.barcelo.com ⏱ 10.00–19.00 daily

Sea Salt Museum

About 5 km from Caleta de Fuste, on the Jandía road, is **Las Salinas**, where the Sea Salt Museum is housed. You will find it difficult to miss, as there is a huge skeleton of a whale outside, and it's a great place to go with children.

Sea salt was first collected in 1861 at Gran Tarajal. An area south of El Castillo soon followed, and in the 20th century Las Salinas del Carmen was started, along with various others dotted around the island, continuing production for a number of years, before falling into disuse due to competition from imported salt. Recently, however – as on the neighbouring island of Lanzarote – there has been a revival in the use of this naturally produced salt. ❸ Las Salinas del Carmen ❶ 928 174 926 ⏱ 10.00–18.00 Tues–Sat; closed Sun & Mon

Shopping

Caleta de Fuste has several shopping centres to explore. Many of these are lively by day, with a good mixture of shops, bars and restaurants; others come to life during the evening, and are the best places for nightlife. There is a large and impressive perfume store operated by Riu Parfum in **El Castillo Commercial Centre** where you can buy every imaginable brand of fragrance.

Tennis

El Castillo Along with regular tennis, the same company also offers mini-golf, paddle tennis (a form of tennis popular in Spain) and basketball. ❸ Barceló Complex (behind the main entrance to the Barceló Hotel, next to the beach) ❶ 928 547 517

Vehicle hire

4x4 Rental A 4WD vehicle can be necessary to reach some of the island's remote beaches and landscapes. Always follow the local restrictions regarding protected areas. The company is based just north of Caleta de Fuste in El Matorral. ⓐ Calle El Trillo 7, Polígono Industrial El Matorral ⓣ 928 163 691/690 923 828 ⓦ www.alquiler-4x4.es

Backtrax Off-Road Motorcycle Tours Offers a variety of 2-hour to full-day bike tours for riders of all experience levels, as well as multi-day riding packages with accommodation. The half-day tour runs to the west of the island and includes a stop on the beach where the SS *American Star* shipwreck lies grounded, as well as a scenic ride through the mountains to Pájara. Quad tours require only a car driving licence, two-wheelers need a bike licence. ⓐ Hotel Elba Castillo Antigua, Avenida José Franchy Roca ⓣ 656 753 055/656 752 528 ⓦ www.backtrax1.com

Buggy Excursions For buggy rentals and guided tourist excursions. ⓐ Villa Florida Apartments 107 ⓣ 928 160 292/638 807 840

Cool Runnings Chauffeur-driven or self-drive trike tours covering various parts of the island. Tours last from two to eight hours. ⓐ Local 4, Amuley Mar Business Centre, Avenida José Franchy Roca ⓣ 928 547 513/649 938 581 ⓦ www.fuertetrikes.com ⓔ coolrunnings@inbox.com

Watersports

Deep Blue Dive School Beginners' introductory course of 3½ hours over three days or a three-full-day course ending with a PADI certificate. ⓐ Hotel Barceló, El Castillo harbour ⓣ 928 163 712 ⓦ www.deep-blue-diving.com ⓛ Daily 08.00–19.00 (summer), 08.00–17.00 (winter)

Escuela de Windsurfing del Castillo Basic windsurfing instruction or advanced courses at El Castillo. ⓣ 928 163 100/101

Sun Sport Offers rental and school for jet-skis, pedal boats, and kayaks.
ⓐ Yacht harbour ❶ 630 758 648 🕐 10.00–17.30 daily

TAKING A BREAK

Panna & Pomodoro £ ❶ Italian ice cream and pizza, both made from the freshest ingredients available make this a popular stop in the shopping mall for lunch or a snack. ⓐ Centro Comercial Atlántico ❶ 928 163 656 🕐 10.00–01.00 Mon–Sat, 11.00–01.00 Sun

Tommy Nutters £ ❷ Serves traditional English food. ⓐ Centro Comercial El Castillo ❶ 619 476 597 🕐 09.00–22.00 daily

El Camarote ££ ❸ Reputedly the best fish restaurant in the area. ⓐ Muelle Deportivo ❶ 928 869 073 🕐 12.00–22.30 daily

🔺 *Caleta de Fuste's sandy beach is safe for children*

Los Caracolitos ££ ❹ Located 5 km (3 miles) south of Caleta (it has a pick-up service at the resorts for customers) in the town of Las Salinas del Carmen, so you can tie in a visit to the Sea Salt Museum. It serves fantastic food, fresh fish, local specialities and has an interesting location overlooking the salt deposits and the sea. ⓐ Las Salinas del Carmen 22 ❶ 928 174 242 ● 12.00–18.00 Mon–Sat, closed Sun

La Frasquita ££ ❺ Specialising in fresh fish, you can select from the catch of the day as it is brought to your table. ⓐ Calle Aulaga 20 ❶ 928 163 657 ● 13.00–16.00, 18.00–22.00 Tues–Sun, closed Mon

Gambrinus ££ ❻ Chain of seafood restaurants found all over Spain. ⓐ Centro Comercial Broncemar Beach, Calle de Ajicán 4 ❶ 928 163 555 ● 10.00–24.00 daily

Mexican Corner ££ ❼ Mexican food. ⓐ Centro Comercial El Castillo ❶ 928 163 460 ● 12.00–23.00 daily

La Paella ££ ❽ Local and international dishes. Watch the sun setting over the bay near the castle. ⓐ Plaza Ingeniero Liste ● 12.30–22.00 daily ❶ Wheelchair access

AFTER DARK

Caleta de Fuste is a family-oriented resort, so expect nightlife to consist of pubs that welcome children. Look for an ever-changing set of bars and occasional discos in the Centro Comercial Atlántico shopping mall, south of town on the way to Las Salinas.

Flower of Scotland ❷ A long cocktail menu, a DJ from 21.00 daily, family-friendly atmosphere and sports on multiple plasma screens make this home away from home for Scots and others. ⓐ Centro Comercial El Castillo ❶ 649 901 371

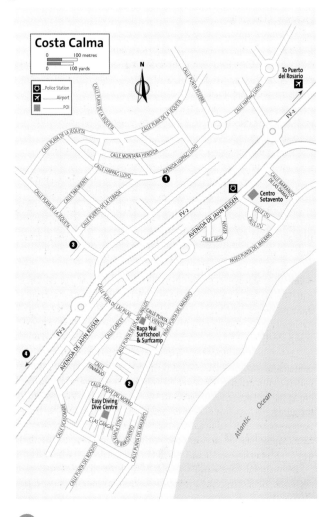

Costa Calma

This is a tranquil family resort on a huge sweep of pale golden sand backed by low cliffs. Elegant houses now mingle with hotels, apartments and commercial centres. On Sunday mornings, a colourful, busy market brings a buzz to the town.

Of course, Costa Calma's fabulous beaches attract an abundance of watersports fans, and every July the area hosts the World Cup windsurfing championships.

The commercial **Centro Sotavento** contains a good selection of restaurants and bars, which come to life in the evening.

The long beach stretches about 1.5 km (1 mile) and is popular with joggers. At one end of the seafront, part of the El Granillo housing scheme, is the beautiful **Hotel Rio Calma** (see page 109). Opened in 2003, the hotel was designed by Basque architect Luis Sánchez. The colonial-style architecture is really eye-catching and everything is of the highest quality. Definitely one of the most impressive hotels on the island, it offers everything you could wish for, from a wellness centre to swimming pools, tennis and squash courts, mini-golf and pitch-and-putt. The gardens are well kept and peaceful – even if you don't stay there, it is worth going to see such an unusual and beautiful building. A range of other hotels and aparthotels are set along the seafront, with most activity centres and windsurf schools located at the south end.

Costa Calma has its own sea-water desalination plant, which was built in 1986 and provides many of the hotels and holiday complexes with water. In addition, waste water is piped to a sewage plant to be processed and re-used as *agua verde*. This recycled water helps to keep the gardens of hotels and complexes lush and green, and enables the avenues of beautiful palms and Canary pines to thrive. Choose this area for its superb beaches, ample tourist facilities and holiday activities, but don't expect to find much local colour or taste of Canarian life here.

A bus goes to Jandía and Morro Jable, which are Costa Calma's neighbouring resorts. This runs hourly, on the half hour (🕐 09.30–21.00 Mon–Sat).

○ *Blue skies over Costa Calma*

THINGS TO SEE & DO

Diving

Easy Diving Diving trips leave the centre at approximately 09.30 and return at 13.00. There is also a flexible afternoon dive. Beginners' diving courses last over five days and include four half-hour dives in open water. Snorkelling trips are also available. ⓐ 200 m (220 yds) from Centro Comercial Botánico, Hotel Morasol, Playa de los Albertos ⓣ 928 876 305/626 285 892 ⓛ 09.00–16.30 Mon–Sat, closed Sun

Rapa Nui Surfschool & Surfcamp This coast is one of the best surfing areas on the island, and courses here cater to beginners and experts alike. ⓐ Centro Comercial Bahía Calma ⓣ 928 549 140/680 888 542 ⓦ www.rapanui-surfschool.com ⓔ info@rapanui-surfschool.com

TAKING A BREAK

Asador de Leña Don Quijote ££ ❶ Known for its tapas and traditional Castilian dishes. The roast suckling pig is outstanding, but served only by advance notice and to groups of six or more. ⓐ Santa Ursula Apartments, Avenida Happag Lloyd ⓣ 928 875 158 ⓛ 18.00–23.00 daily

Galería ££ ❷ German-run restaurant, serving a variety of Mediterranean food and pasta dishes. ⓐ Calle Risco Blanco s/n ⓣ 928 875 416 ⓦ www. restaurant-galeria.com ⓛ 18.00–23.00 Tues–Sun, closed Mon

Restaurante Copa ££ ❸ German-owned with well-prepared food. Children can draw on the paper tablecloths. ⓐ Centro Comercial El Palmeral ⓣ 646 755 305 ⓛ 18.00–22.00 Tues–Sun, closed Mon

La Terraza del Gato ££ ❹ Stylish international dishes and Canarian specialities are prepared with fresh ingredients at this chic terrace overlooking the sea, in the classy Risco del Gato Hotel. ⓐ Calle Sicasumbre ⓣ 928 547 030 ⓛ 12.00–24.00 daily

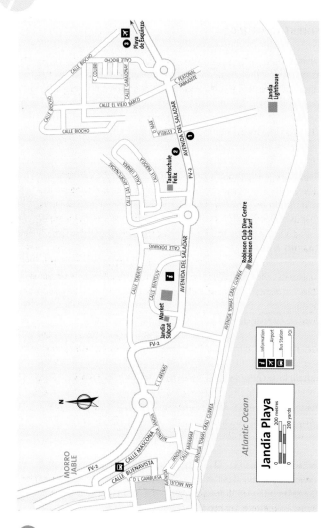

Jandía Playa

Atlantic Ocean

0 ___ 200 metres
0 ___ 200 yards

Information
Airport
Bus Station
POI

Jandía Playa

Jandía Playa is in the very south of Fuerteventura, two or three kilometres (a couple of miles) to the east of Morro Jable (see page 49). Its beach (known by locals as Playa del Matorral) is a magnet for watersports enthusiasts.

THINGS TO SEE & DO

Bikes
Fuertebike A telephone call is all that is needed for this excursion. Everyone is picked up and taken by car to visit Betancuria and the journey then continues by bike to the coastal village of Ajuy for a picnic on the beach. You are then transported up the hill and continue by bike to La Pared, a 10-km (6-mile) downhill run, from where you're driven back to your starting point (pick-up and set-down at Costa Calma too). Another trip is available for those who want a more challenging ride, plus some walking and cave exploration. ❶ 629 362 795 Ⓦ www.fuertebike.com ❸ fuerte-bike@yahoo.de ❶ Mon, Wed, Thur, Fri & Sat

Boat-based activities
For the best views of the Jandía coast and the lighthouse, board one of the many excursion boats leaving from the harbour at Morro Jable.

Jandía Subcat The trip takes approximately 90 minutes and the sub dives up to 30-m (100-ft) deep. You will see a myriad of different fish, both large and small, if you are lucky. ❸ Avenida del Saladar, Local 36 ❶ 928 166 392/629 153 583/900 507 006 Ⓦ www.subcat-fuerteventura.com ❶ Tues–Fri ❶ Charge for trip

Watersports
Tauchschule Felix This dive centre organises two diving trips per day for experienced divers. ❸ Avenida del Saladar 9 ❶ 928 541 418 Ⓦ www.tauchen-fuerteventura.com

◯ *Watersports are very popular at Jandía Playa*

Robinson Club Dive Centre This reliable diving centre with outpost on the beach (see map on page 44) covers all levels of abilities. Twice a week there is a children's course in the pool. Every diver needs a licence, log book, medical certificate and insurance. 🄰 Office: Avenida del Saladar 6 🄣 928 541 065/928 169 538 🄻 Guided dives 09.00 & 14.00 daily; night dives on Wed ❶ Minimum age for sea dives is 12

Robinson Club Surf Offers beginners' surfing courses lasting between 10 and 12 hours. Board rental is available. 🄰 Office: Avenida del Saladar 6 🄣 928 169 100 🅦 www.robinson-ep.com

TAKING A BREAK

Boot and Ball Sports Bar ££ ❶ British-style food, hot and cold snacks, Sunday roast from midday. Children's mini-cine. Big-screen TV with all major sports shown live. 🄰 Avenida del Saladar 17 🄻 10.30 onwards

Don Pedro ££ ❷ Unlike most in Jandía, this is a traditional Canarian/ Spanish restaurant, and it has a non-smoking section. 🄰 Avenida del Saladar 🄣 928 541 825

Restaurante Marabú ££ ❸ A good Spanish restaurant, very popular with the locals. Ten-minute drive from Jandía Playa. 🄰 Calle Fuente de Hija 2, Playa de Esquinzo 🄣 928 544 098 🅦 www.e-marabu.com 🄻 13.00–23.00 Mon–Sat, closed Sun

RESORTS

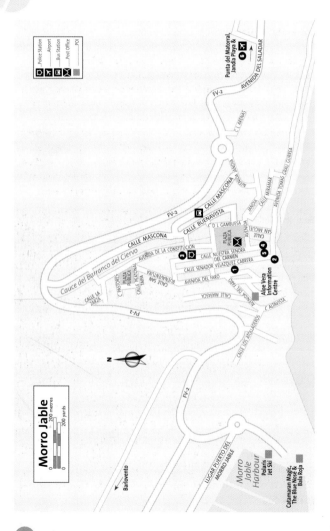

Morro Jable

It is hard to believe that this was once another small fishing village, in what was a remote part of the island. Situated in the island's south, it has become one of the largest holiday centres on Fuerteventura. There is something for everyone: sea, beaches, hotels, apartments, commercial centres, restaurants, bars, shops and a marina.

The remains of the old village lie on the slopes of a *barranco* (a steep hillside), where the fishermen still go in and out of the harbour. The lighthouse situated on the **Punta del Matorral** marks the most southerly point of Fuerteventura. Inland, towards the mountains, there is the wild and unspoilt countryside of **northern Jandía**, a paradise for walkers.

⬥ *Morro Jable*

◓ *Make friends with a donkey in Parque Natural de Jandía*

To the east of Morro Jable lies Jandía Playa (known as Playa del Matorral), with its breathtakingly beautiful, pale-golden sandy beaches bordering a stunning, crystal-clear turquoise sea (see page 45).

Much of the peninsula, with its rugged mountains, is a conservation area and forms part of the **Parque Natural de Jandía**. In some of the remote mountain valleys it is still possible to see wild goats and donkeys.

The longest beaches with the highest waves are to be found in Jandía, making it a must for surfers and windsurfers – winds here can reach up to Force 9! On the northwestern side of Jandía is the secluded beach of **Barlovento**, popular with scuba divers and naturists.

THINGS TO SEE & DO

Aloe Vera Information Centre
Visit the Aloe Vera Information Centre where you can learn more about the growing and processing of this locally produced plant, and sample some of the potions and lotions. ⓐ Avenida del Faro 10 ⓘ 928 166 329 ⓔ Aloe-vera-canarias@web.de

Boat-based activities
Catamaran Magic This is run by a company that also operates in Ibiza and Gran Canaria. The trip includes a light meal of chicken, salad, potatoes and *mojo* (a spicy, typical Canarian sauce, see page 85), plus two drinks (water, soft drinks, beer and wine). The boat cruises along the coastline on the look-out for dolphins and other marine life. ⓐ Morro Jable harbour ⓘ 900 506 260/928 150 248 ⓛ Trips daily from 10.30–14.00

Polaris Jet Ski Sessions start every two hours from 08.00 to 18.00 and last for 90 minutes. Life jackets are supplied. ⓐ Morro Jable harbour ⓘ 616 437 184/639 706 930 ⓛ Mon–Sat, closed Sun

Fishing
The Blue Nose Big-game fishing, with food and drinks included. ⓐ Morro Jable harbour ⓘ 628 021 451 ⓛ Two five-hour trips daily

Sea excursions

Bala Roja This large Zodiac® will take you to beaches and coves that cannot be accessed by land. ☎ 928 541 771 ❶ Booking by phone

TAKING A BREAK

Refugio £ ❶ Cheap local bar with good tapas. ⓐ Calle Senador Velázquez Cabrera 3

Leos ££ ❷ Lovely atmosphere, and right by the sea – you can sit and watch the world go by. Family-run business serving good food, including fresh fish. ⓐ Avenida del Mar 25 ☎ 928 540 724 🕙 10.00–23.00 daily

Piccola Italia ££ ❸ A really good Italian restaurant, with excellent pizza and pasta. ⓐ Calle Nuestra Señora del Carmen 39 ☎ 928 541 258 🕙 13.00–16.00, 19.00–24.00 Wed–Mon, closed Thur

Posada San Borondón ££ ❹ A characterful restaurant decorated as a ship, so you can't miss it! Serves mainly Spanish food, with *flambés* a speciality. Live music at the weekends adds to the atmosphere. ⓐ Plaza de Cirilo López ☎ 928 541 428 🕙 18.00–02.00 Mon–Sat, closed Sun

Restaurante Charly ££ ❺ This long-established restaurant always has good food, with fresh fish a speciality. ⓐ Plaza de Cirilo López (near the taxi rank) ☎ 928 541 066

Restaurante Coronado £££ ❻ A sophisticated restaurant with a good ambience, a place to go for that special, romantic dinner. Excellent service, international cuisine. ⓐ Apartments Coronado, between the Riu Calypso and the Hotel Riu Palace, El Sol 14 ☎ 928 541 440 ⓦ www.restaurantecoronado.es 🕙 Thur–Tues 19.00–23.00 (until 23.30 Fri–Sun)

❿ *Wide open spaces in Fuerteventura's hinterland*

EXCURSIONS
Out & about

Northern Fuerteventura

Lajares

Just ten minutes' drive from Corralejo, this somewhat rambling village is well worth a visit to watch the local women making their traditional openwork embroidery. Exquisitely crafted, the finished items are for sale in the shop marked **Artesanía de Lajares** where you can buy tablecloths, napkins, shirts and aprons, together with other small embroidered items. There are also many souvenirs for sale including some hand-painted pottery. ☎ 928 868 300 ✉ artesanialajares@gmail.com 🕐 09.00–19.00 Mon–Fri, 09.00–13.00 Sat, closed Sun

The village is also notable for its wrestling arena, in which the traditional Lucha Canaria (a form of wrestling, a bit like Sumo) takes place.

Try **Pizzeria La Cancela**, for great pizzas made in a kiln. The restaurant is in a lovely restored traditional house. ➌ Calle Central 2, near the roundabout ☎ 928 868 568 🕐 09.00–23.00 daily

La Oliva

Sixteen kilometres (10 miles) south of Corralejo lies La Oliva, a part-old part-new town, the centrepiece of which is the church of **Nuestra Señora de la Candelaria** (Our Lady of Candelaria). An impressive building, the church's white walls contrast starkly with the square bell tower built of black volcanic stone.

On the outskirts of town there is a very interesting building called **La Casa de los Coroneles** (The House of the Colonels), built at the beginning of the 18th century for the military forces who wielded great power at that time. It is a fortress-like manor house, with its wooden balconies, doors and shutters decorated with carvings. Above the entrance is the coat of arms of the Cabrera family, with a crown, a tree and a goat. 🕐 10.00–18.00 Tues–Sat, closed Sun & Mon

Between the church and Casa de los Coroneles, look for the **Centro de Arte Canario**, one of the islands' foremost galleries and collections of

⬥ *Nuestra Señora de la Candelaria*

contemporary Canarian art. Permanent and temporary exhibits include sculpture displayed in the gardens. ⓐ Calle Salvador Manrique de Lara ① 928 868 233 ⓔ centrodeartecanario2@gmail.com ① 10.00–17.00 Mon–Sat (until 18.00 June–Sept)

Tindaya

Driving south from La Oliva, the village of Tindaya lies at the base of **Montaña Tindaya**, from the peak of which on a clear day you can see across to Mount Teide on Tenerife, which is Spain's highest mountain.

Because of its unusually light marble colour, Montaña Tindaya used to be regarded by the islanders as a religious place. They left behind a large number of outlines of feet carved into the rock which were said to keep away the evil spirits. On the drive from La Oliva or El Cotillo the almost white mountain stands out from the others of ochre and terracotta. Eduardo Chillida, a well-known Basque sculptor in the last century, wanted to hollow out the mountain, making it into a work of art in its own right. If you want to climb the mountain you have to get written permission at the Cabildo Insular, Puerto del Rosario, or their office in Corralejo.

In the village itself there is a rather lavishly appointed little church, a football pitch, an English bar and a few Spanish ones, and a very successful cheese factory. The bars are mostly used by the locals, so you will find their prices compare very well with those found in the resort establishments.

Tefía

On the same road, heading towards Antigua, the village of Tefía houses the **Ecomuseo de la Alcogida**, a reconstruction of seven typical old Fuerteventuran houses. The museum gives one of the Canaries' best pictures of how life used to be before tourism changed the local economy. You can see how a well-to-do family would have lived. There is also an example of a more modest family house, and there are two showing the way of life of artisans. Traditional handicrafts are demonstrated (and sold), and there are exhibitions, a film show and a bar. The everyday necessities of village life had to be made locally, so there are workshops illustrating how carpenters, metalworkers, potters and stonemasons supplied all that was needed for domestic use. You can also see breadmaking (and sample the results), openwork embroidery and weaving. There is a restaurant, too. ☎ 928 175 343 🕐 10.00–18.00 Tues–Sat, closed Sun & Mon

Los Molinos

Los Molinos is west of Tefía, signposted 'Las Parcelas'. This hamlet is one of the few remaining out-of-the-way refuges for local people. There is no electricity, and no clean running water. Mobile phones are also out of range. Five or six caravans are permanently parked here, beside a huddle of a dozen or so small fishermen's houses which are only occupied during the summer months. There is space for two or three cars, and room for a few more on the other side of a stream for those brave enough to attempt the ford.

The black sand and pebble beach is bordered on either side by rocks from which the fishermen cast their lines. In summer, this beach is golden. Fish is the order of the day in the restaurant shack – you can choose from whatever has just been caught. A terrace supplies much-needed shade from the sun.

Casillas del Ángel

About 12 km (7½ miles) west of Puerto del Rosario on the Betancuria road is a small, attractive and spread-out village of old houses. In the village, visit La Casa de los Rugama and the church, both clearly marked on the main road. Also on the main road, **Restaurante La Era de Casillas** is a beautiful traditional house that serves Canarian specialities. ☎ 928 538 348 🕐 13.00–16.30, 20.00–24.00 Tues–Sun, closed Mon

Central Fuerteventura

Antigua

For just one year (between 1835 and 1836), Antigua was the island's capital. However, it was not economically viable, and La Oliva, further north, became the capital until 1860, when the honour was given to Puerto del Rosario. The little town of Antigua, now the administrative centre for several surrounding villages, is a mixture of old and modern buildings, the most noticeable being the new town hall and police station. Opposite these two is the church of **Nuestra Señora de Antigua** (Our Lady of Antigua), which was built in 1785 and has a beautifully carved teak roof – especially over the altar which is colourful and gently gilded. The church is on one side of an attractive square which has a number of old trees.

In May or June every year folklore groups and craftspeople from all over the islands meet to demonstrate their skills and sell their products at the **Feria Insular de Artesanía**, which is held on the outskirts of the town. ❶ 928 878 004

On the road to La Ampuyenta there is a well-restored windmill, **Molino de Antigua**, which was used to grind barley. Climb to the top to see the wooden cogs and gears. In addition, the mill site features gardens, archaeological and art exhibits, a restaurant and an outstanding craft shop. The road to this centre has street lights shaped like old lanterns. ❶ 10.00–18.00 Tues–Sat, closed Sun & Mon

Betancuria

Betancuria is tucked away in the hills. It is atmospheric and tranquil, with stunning views as you approach it over the mountains. This enchanting little village, just over 11 km (7 miles) from Antigua and the oldest in the Canary Islands, was the island's capital for many years when it was first colonised. Considering that Fuerteventura is a desert island, you pass a surprising amount of vegetation, including dragos, the unusual trees that are indigenous to the Canaries, and in the past were believed to have magical qualities. There is a *mirador* (viewpoint) north of town, with 360-degree views and a restaurant designed by Lanzarote artist César Manrique.

Betancuria itself, nestling among the mountains, has a decidedly peaceful air about it. The site was chosen by Jean de Béthencourt as a safe place, difficult for the pirates to find. However, this proved not to be the case, for in 1593 pirates pillaged the town, destroying everything and capturing many of the inhabitants for slavery. Its church was not rebuilt until the 17th century.

On the drive down to the village, still on the outskirts, there is an attractive roofless building on the left, the ruin of an old Franciscan monastery that was abandoned on the orders of Queen Isabella II of Spain in 1837. It fell into disrepair, although this is not the reason for the absence of the roof, which was dismantled and sold for grain and water during an exceptionally bad drought in the last century. No one, however, seems to remember the exact details! Until it was abandoned, the monks developed their evangelical work and promoted education, the monastery acting as a place of learning.

The **Iglesia de Santa María** (Church of St Mary) was first consecrated in the year 1410. In 1426 it was elevated to become a cathedral and bishopric, although no bishop ever came to take up the post. It contains a number of interesting items, all of which are explained during the half-hourly guided tours.

There is a small, interesting **archaeological museum** in Betancuria. 🕐 10.00–18.00 Tues–Sat, closed Sun & Mon

At **Casa Santa María**, a lovingly restored old house with exposed beams, is a charming patio where you can buy drinks, ice cream and snacks. The restaurant inside has won Spanish awards for its gastronomy. 🅰 Plaza Santa Maria 📞 928 878 282 🕐 11.00–17.00, 20.00–23.00 daily

Valle de Santa Inés

The 17th-century church in Valle de Santa Inés, near Betancuria, contains a Baroque altar and five notable paintings. In the village centre are a restaurant, bar, supermarket and craft shop. The bar is used by the villagers and offers tapas and fine local cheese.

On the outskirts of the village is the **Taller de Artesanía Cerámica**, a handmade pottery workshop. Ceramics are produced here by various members of one family, headed by Doña Josefa, in a style unique to Fuerteventura. The methods and colouring have been handed down

◆ *Iglesia de Santa María, Betancuria*

through the generations. Doña Josefa's sister works close by, patiently producing traditional straw hats. There are few people these days who are prepared to cut and dry the young palm leaves, split them into required widths, plait them, and then laboriously sew each section into a hat shape.

Aguas Verdes

Aguas Verdes, on the west coast, is a good place to fish from the rocks, if you don't mind a twisting, turning rough-road drive to get here. Take the road to Betancuria and fork right at Llanos de la Concepción. The road follows the river bed, which only flows during the winter months but retains sufficient moisture to sustain the tamarisk trees. You drive through rolling, ochre hills, past a hotel on your left, then continue on down past a few newly built houses to a pebble beach. Apart from the odd tent it is fairly quiet here.

La Ampuyenta

La Ampuyenta is a village in the centre of Fuerteventura, close to both Antigua and Betancuria. The chancel in the village's parish church is decorated with murals. **Casa Mena La Ampuyenta** is a well-kept, typical village house dating from the 19th century. It was owned by a successful local doctor, born in 1802, who studied and practised in various other islands and countries and specialised in tropical diseases, a topic upon which he frequently lectured. Mena was a true philanthropist who left money to the village to build a hospital, not far away from his house. However, although the hospital was built, there was never enough money actually to run it, and so it stands empty and unused. It seems a pity that his house does not have any of the doctor's implements to give us an insight into the 'tools of the trade' of that era. ◷ 10.00–18.00 Tues–Sun, closed Mon

For a fabulous meal, book ahead for a table at **Restaurante Fabiola**. ☏ 928 174 605 ◷ Thur–Sat dinner, Sun lunch, closed Mon–Wed

Pájara

This town is about 10 km (6 miles) south of Betancuria. It is the administrative centre of the largest of the island's six municipalities, reaching way down to Morro Jable and the southern tip of the island. The town itself has an enticing shady square surrounded by Indian laurel trees and flowering shrubs, and there is a constant chattering of birds.

The square features a *noria* (bucket pump) that shows how donkeys, camels – or, when necessary, man drew water from the ground in the days before electric pumps. The church, **Nuestra Señora de la Regla**, built in 1687, has a most unusual door surround, believed to be influenced by Aztec designs. Inside it is wide with sturdy columns down the centre. It has an unusual double altarpiece, both of which are colourful, the left one having floral recesses and doors. There is a beautifully decorated pulpit.

Not far from the square you will find a **Craft Centre** where you can see demonstrations of traditional openwork embroidery and weaving. Many local products are for sale here. 🕐 10.00–13.00 Mon, Tues, Thur & Fri, 11.00–12.00 & 15.00–18.00 Wed; closed Sat, Sun & fiestas

For traditional cuisine using locally grown organic ingredients, stop at Casa Isaitas. 🛈 928 161 402 🕐 10.00–22.00 daily (July–Sept); 10.00–18.00 daily (Oct–June)

The coast west of Pájara is a wild and desolate one, with soaring headlands, sea caves and pounding surf. It was here that the decommissioned ship SS *American Star* broke loose from the vessel that was towing it and crashed ashore in a storm in 1994. It still lies rusting away just offshore, with surf spouting through its portholes. You can reach this wild coast by car, although the dirt track is rough. It is a favourite route for quad- and motorised bike excursions from Caleta de Fuste (see Backtrax Off-Road Motorcycle Tours, page 37).

Ajuy

If a gentle day out is what you want, then take the Ajuy road northwest from Pájara. Ajuy is about 11 km (7 miles) along a sleepy valley of

🔺 *Aztec-influenced door at Nuestra Señora de la Regla church in Pájara*

agricultural land, following the path of a wide river bed. En route you'll see many tomato sheds (tomatoes are an important part of the island economy) that seem to blend into the countryside, since they are made of sacking the same colour as the earth. There are numerous 'wigwams' erected in the fields or near houses – these are canes put up to dry, ready to be used for staking the tomato plants.

Ajuy itself lies on a black sandy beach and is a mixture of old dwellings and new buildings. It is a small resort, away from the bustle and noise of the island's other resorts. There is a choice of three or four restaurants, all of which serve fish caught on the day. Be bold and try some, even if they are unrecognisable; you can't get fresher than this.

The sea can be rough, so take care bathing. On the plus side, here and all along the west coast, you experience the wildness and power of nature. The rocky seabed and underwater caves are a scuba diver's paradise. On the north side of Ajuy is a path that snakes around the cliff-side and leads to most unusual sponge-like rock formations, and on to a bay containing a dozen or so little fishing boats. One expects houses around the next corner, but in fact you find a semicircle of caves, giving you a chance to explore one of the oldest inhabited parts of the island.

Vega del Río Palmas

Vega, south of Betancuria, is a small and quite insignificant village at first sight, but there is a lot more to it than first meets the eye. The **church** (🕐 11.00–13.00 Tues–Fri, closed Mon; Mass on Sat 18.00) was built in 1660 and houses a statue of **La Virgen de la Peña**, believed to have been brought by Jean de Béthencourt and placed in the church of Betancuria. When Betancuria was ransacked the local people managed to hide the sculpture, which they did so well that it wasn't rediscovered until the 17th century – in Vega! The Virgin is the patron saint of the Canary Isles, and every year on the third Saturday in September, people come to Vega del Río Palmas from all over the island, in a pilgrimage (see page 106) to celebrate with a magnificent procession followed by a fiesta. A little way past the church a road to the right takes you alongside the river bed and through the rest of the village. Verdant, unspoilt and dotted with old houses, there are probably more animals here than people. Little terraced fields abound, with lush oases consisting of palm trees, bamboo cane and shrubs.

Follow this same road to Las Peñitas, where among the huge boulders you will see metal watermills working to pump up the water from underground. There is both fresh and saline water: the latter is only good for watering tomatoes, while the former is used for both irrigation and drinking. There are at least two *norias* (bucket pumps) – turned at one time by donkeys or camels – now either in disuse or functioning with the help of a motor. At the end of this there is a reservoir that is

⬤ *The coastal path at Ajuy*

surrounded by reeds and tamarisks, a haven for frogs and birds. All these things are expected in Europe, but remember – this is a desert island!

Do stop for a meal at **Don Antonio**, or at least a coffee or a glass of wine on the patio of this now beautifully renovated former ruin. Although well kept, the outer appearance of this restaurant does not prepare you for the delights inside. ● Plaza de la Peña, Vega del Río Palmas ● 667 513 713 ● 11.00–17.00 Tues–Sun, evenings by reservation only; closed Mon; also closed in June and the second week in December

Pozo Negro

Pozo Negro on the east coast is an expanding fishing village of colourful houses – the sea comes right up to the waterside houses at high tide. The sea itself can be very rough here, so be careful if you enter the water.

● One of Fuerteventura's traditional windmills

CENTRAL FUERTEVENTURA

Every two years in May **Pozo Negro** is home of **La Feaga**, a kind of 'county show' Fuerteventura-style. If you want an island excursion with a difference, this is the place to go. There's everything from the Goat Supreme Championships, Lucha (Canarian wrestling), horse racing, cheese-making and arts and crafts for sale. The show lasts for four days, and be prepared to eat your fill of local food samples. There is also a tree nursery at the site of La Feaga, and a nursery which grows experimental crops of tomatoes, potatoes and onions.

Just off the main road down to the village, you will see buildings used for the Feaga (see box above).

Not far from the village, a short stretch of tarmacked road (that quickly becomes a track) takes you down to the remains of a **prehistoric village**. This settlement consisted of 100 or so crudely built primitive houses. Most of them are in poor condition, but one of them has been reconstructed to give us an idea of what they were originally like. A trail leads from the settlement up a cone-shaped hill for a good overview of the site. There are more, similar house remains scattered between here and the coast, often near the site of springs for fresh water.

For a reviving meal of fresh fish or paella try **Los Pescadores**, right on the waterfront. ☎ 928 174 653 🕐 12.00–21.30 daily

Tiscamanita

Tiscamanita, on the road south of Antigua towards Tuineje, is well worth a visit. In the village square, there stands a black marble monument to **Manuel Velázquez Cabrera**, the father of the island's government. Nearby, and close to St Mark's Church, there stands an interesting old crenellated tithe barn in which villagers at one time stored their 10 per cent contribution towards the church's upkeep.

67

The region is steeped in the traditions of agriculture, producing fields of aloe vera, ecologically grown and processed for the modern market. At nightfall, Egyptian vultures, protected birds, roost on the electricity pylons beside the roads. Perfect examples of extinct volcanoes are everywhere, all with names. There is a series of volcanic tubes where some of the ancient inhabitants dwelt.

Just outside the village there is the fascinating **Centro de Interpretacion Los Molinos** (Windmill Centre), with a peaceful and pretty courtyard. The history of milling in Fuerteventura is presented, and explained by the helpful, knowledgeable and multilingual curator. This mill produced *gofio*, a finely ground flour made of roasted corn or wheat that is a central feature of Canarian cuisine (see page 84). It is used as a garnish, and in cooking to thicken soups and stews. It is also used to coat some varieties of *majorero* goat's cheese (see page 86), adding a toasted flavour. Milling maize was a social occasion and an opportunity to meet up with other families. ☎ 928 164 275 🕐 09.30–17.30 Tues–Fri & Sun, closed Mon & Sat

Tuineje

An agricultural town, south of Tiscamanita, Tuineje is the administrative centre for eight villages. It sits in a nature reserve which also contains the volcanic peaks La Caldera de Gairia and Los Cuchillos de Vigán. The wide valleys between these two support very little vegetation, but the park is a safe place for several endangered species of birds.

Tuineje's church is quite splendid. Completed in 1790, it is dedicated to San Miguel Arcangel. Every 13 October the town celebrates its victory in 1740 against the English pirates who attacked Fuerteventura. The event is recorded in two paintings in the church, built in the late 1700s.

The light and the landscape in this area is so unusual that many filmmakers and advertising companies choose it as a set for their works.

Southern Fuerteventura

Las Playitas

Las Playitas, southeast of Tuineje and 6 km (3½ miles) northeast of Gran
Tarajal, reminds the visitor of what Fuerteventura used to be like.
A few fishermen's cottages border the black sandy beach, on which
their sun-bleached and sea-faded boats are pulled up. There is a small
harbour with a slipway. Among the winding alleyways there are a few
restaurants, mostly serving very fresh fish. Should you decide to stay
the night, there is accommodation in the village, and if you ask in one
of the bars or restaurants they are only too willing to help.

Just outside the village, a narrow winding tarmac road leads to the
most unusual and amazing lighthouse, **El Faro de la Entallada**, high up
on the mountain. It was built in 1953 as a fort with an inner courtyard.
The masonry is of black stones with white mortar and red edges. You
can walk around outside and will be mesmerised by the crashing waves
on the rocks far below. This is not a trip for the faint-hearted or those
who suffer from vertigo!

Gran Tarajal

Just southwest of Las Playitas, Gran Tarajal is the second-largest town
on the island, with a blue-flag beach of black sand. Gran Tarajal has a
long and quite handsome promenade where you can sit with a beer,
a coffee or an ice cream and watch the world go by.

For some years now more trade has passed through this port
than through Puerto del Rosario, the capital, and during the winter
months it is still very busy with the transportation and export of
tomatoes. A lot of building and modernising has changed the town,
but one fragment of history that remains is the thick-trunked palm
grove growing in the town centre, which was planted generations ago
to protect crops from the cruel winds. Today this is where the town's
health centre is located.

⬤ *The untouched village of Las Playitas (see page 69)*

Although today we may no longer understand the importance of lime, it was not too long ago that lime was invaluable, especially as a building material. A huge kiln was built in 1953 on a 6,000 sq m (7,175 sq yd) piece of rural land near Gran Tarajal, with a workshop and accommodation for the workforce. Processed lime was then mixed with water and used both for whitewashing and constructing houses.

During the last fortnight of August, Gran Tarajal hosts a Youth Festival, while in September, since 1995, there has been an annual international fishing competition for big-game fish such as blue and white marlin. Once caught and weighed, the fish are tagged and returned to the sea.

Gran Tarajal Auditorium

An important island venue for concerts and dances. ☎ 928 162 449
🕐 Only open for performances

TAKING A BREAK

Confradía de Pescadores ££ Local restaurant serving fresh fish.
📍 Recinto Portuario ☎ 928 162 074 🕐 08.00–23.00 Mon–Sat,
08.00–17.00 Sun

Da Nonna Diana ££ Traditional Italian cuisine is on the menu here.
📍 Avenida Paco Hierro 6 ☎ 928 162 339 🕐 09.00–02.00 Thur–Tues,
closed Wed

Restaurante Avenida Italia ££ Specialising in Italian cuisine. 📍 Avenida
Paco Hierro 9 ☎ 928 162 209 🕐 11.00–24.00 Thur–Tues, closed Wed

Restaurante Balandro ££ Fresh fish and meat. 📍 Avenida Paco Hierro 8
☎ 928 162 359 🕐 12.00–16.00, 17.00–24.00 Wed–Mon, closed Tues

Restaurante Chino Oso Panda ££ Chinese cooking. 📍 Calle Atis Tirma 11
☎ 928 162 526 🕐 12.00–16.30, 19.00–24.00 daily

Giniginamar

This delightful little fishing village with a black sandy beach is 4 km (2½ miles) off the main coastal road and southwest of Gran Tarajal. Giniginamar is totally unspoilt, and a reminder of what many of the tourist resorts used to be like before they were commercialised. This protected 'area of biological interest' is a good place to dive. There are a couple of discreetly modernised apartments for holiday lets, and a nicely situated bar-cum-restaurant called **Olas del Sur** with a few tables outside, overlooking the sea. ⓐ Calle del Carmen 5

Tarajalejo

Further down the coast, this little fishing village, on the east coast of the Jandía Peninsula, is at the end of a palm-covered valley. It has a fine, black-sand beach and a small harbour. Apart from the small aquarium (**El Centro de Ocio El Brasero** ⓐ Carretera General Tarajalejo ① 928 161 182 ① 10.00–20.00 Tues–Sun, closed Mon), the village is really only notable for the sports facilities that have become established here, making it a day-out venue for many holidaymakers.

THINGS TO SEE & DO

Horse riding
The **Centro Hípico**, based at El Centro de Ocio (see above), offers horse riding and trekking. ① 928 161 351
Another choice is **Centro Hípico Tarajalejo**. ⓐ Carretera General Tarajalejo ① 928 161 351

Karting
There is a kart track in the village of Cardón, just to the north of Tarajalejo. ① 639 693 984 ⓦ http://kartingfuerteventura.com ① 10.00–20.00 daily

La Lajita

La Lajita is a coastal village inhabited mainly by local people, a few minutes' drive off the main coastal road southwest of Giniginamar and Tarajalejo. Largely unspoilt, the village merits a visit just to have a swim, a coffee or even a meal. However, the main attraction for most visitors is the zoo, **La Lajita Oasis Park**. Set amidst lush tropical gardens, including a cactus garden, the park is home to a wide variety of birds, reptiles, primates and other mammals. Twice-daily parrot shows, along with reptile and birds-of-prey shows, add to camel rides to keep all ages interested. The bar and restaurant have rustic wooden tables and benches beneath palm-leaf sunshades. ⓐ Carretera General de Jandía s/n ❶ 928 400 434 ❶ 928 343 047 Ⓦ www.fuerte-venturaoasispark.com ⓛ 09.30–18.00 daily ❶ Admission charge

La Pared

This small village on the southwest coast of Fuerteventura is notable for its multicoloured beaches. To the south, **La Playa del Viejo Rey** is golden sand; immediately north is **La Playa de la Pared**, made of pebbly, black volcanic sand. La Pared (which means The Wall) is said to have marked the boundary in days gone by between two rival kingdoms, the Maxorata and Jandía. Now, however, nothing remains of the wall except the myth. The coast is one of sheltered bays and extensive dunes, although the sea can be a little rough. Major roads in the area are paved, but access to the beaches is often by dirt tracks.

THINGS TO SEE & DO

Adrenalin Surfschool
This school offers courses at all levels and ages from eight upwards. Prices include all gear and a shuttle service from the resort areas. ⓐ Valle Ancho 12, La Pared ❶ 928 949 034/661 936 484/661 936 490 Ⓦ www.adrenalin-surfschool.com ⓛ 10.00–13.00, 15.00–19.00 daily

⬥ *Take a long, long walk on Cofete's pristine sands*

Rancho Barranco de los Caballos

These riding stables organise two-hour riding excursions for adults and children aged over 10 (must be able to ride). Pick-up is available if you're less than 30 km (18 miles) away. ⓐ Finca Puerto Nuevo ⓣ 928 174 151/619 275 389 ⓦ www.reiten-fuerte.de ⓛ 10.00–12.00, 16.00–18.00 daily

TAKING A BREAK

Restaurant/Bar Bahía Mar

This child-friendly restaurant has a panoramic view of the coast and is wonderful for a family day out. The fish on the menu is straight from the sea below. ⓛ 12.00–16.00, 18.00–22.00 daily

Cofete

To reach Cofete, take the winding road from Morro Jable across the Jandía Peninsula and travel on about 20 km (12 miles) of track that only allows for single-file traffic in some places. It is best to do this in a 4WD vehicle. The village is in an isolated part of Fuerteventura in the mountain mass of Jandía, the peak of which, Pico de la Zarza, is the highest point of the island at 807 m (2,648 ft).

The area is a nature reserve, and has the most wonderful views of the island; on a really clear day you can see other islands to the west. This is a superb area in which to go walking or trekking, but remember to take plenty of water with you – and protection from the sun. Also, let someone know your plans. You will find yourself at one with nature, with only the sound of birdsong, the wind and the waves – it's definitely a place to get away from it all, clear the mind and calm the body. Down on the coast, you can walk and walk on the extensive pristine sands. There is a tiny fishing village there, with a restaurant well known for its fish stew. The beaches are frequently deserted and spectacularly beautiful, with wild seas and often dangerous breakers crashing onto the shore. As the sea recedes, you will find small birds darting about looking for food brought in by the tide.

Hidden in these wild surroundings is the house of **Gustav Winter**, which has many varying myths surrounding it. Winter was a German scientist who escaped from World War II Germany to Fuerteventura, where he laboriously built his unique hideaway, bringing in all the building materials by donkey and camel. There are rumours of secret tunnels leading to his house, but these have never been substantiated. Some say he was a true benefactor, giving money to local nuns to ensure the children had one good meal a day; and that he was responsible for bringing the first electricity to the island. Other rumours paint a darker image of a man who used this fortress-like villa as a refuge for top Nazis. Whatever the truth, the fact remains that a visit to this secluded villa is worth the difficult journey.

The Jandía Peninsula

This area, which includes the resorts of Costa Calma and Morro Jable, is a nature reserve of great beauty and variety. The Parque Natural de Jandía covers 2,688 hectares (6,642 acres) and ranges from the incredibly white sand beaches lapped by turquoise seas on the east coast, to the wilder seas around the west coast's rocky shores. Between the two coasts are hilly ranges, plateaus and plains. This remarkably varied environment is home to much of the island's wildlife, including a number of species of birds of prey and night birds, such as owls. A salt-marsh area entices birds such as dunlin, and there are several specialised plant communities. The

The striking coast of the Jandía Peninsula

PARK REGULATIONS

Remember that it is prohibited in the Jandía Natural Park to:

- Light fires
- Leave rubbish
- Collect any of the plant species
- Camp or use vehicles outside the authorised areas

highest peak is Pico de la Zarza at 807 m (2,648 ft), which is often covered by clouds creating a humid microclimate.

If walking is on your agenda, the hills and valleys of Jandía offer an enormous range of scenery, with spectacular vistas of both sea and land. Silence prevails here, broken only by the cry of the birds or the whistling of the wind.

The beaches on the east coast seem to go on for ever and can be over 1 km (½ mile) wide in some places. Here you can guarantee you will be able to find your own special piece of paradise among the little coves. Do remember, if you are on these isolated beaches, to take plenty of water to drink, and don't forget protection from the sun. You will not find bars or restaurants in the wilder areas, just sand, sea and surf.

While the surf and beaches along this coast are spectacular, they are also exceedingly dangerous to surfers and swimmers. It is best to enjoy this beach from the land and choose somewhere else to challenge the sea.

Lanzarote

A day trip to Lanzarote, Fuerteventura's neighbour to the north, is a major attraction. The smaller island is just 40 minutes away on a pleasant sea crossing. The following organised excursions have pick-up points at Corralejo and El Cotillo. Ask in your hotel or apartments, or see your tour rep, for times and the nearest pick-up point. Many inclusive trips also take in a visit to tiny, unspoilt Isla de Lobos, which is just 3 km (2 miles) offshore from Corralejo.

THINGS TO SEE & DO

Isla de Lobos (Island of Seals)

This lovely island is small, just 470 hectares (1,161 acres), and the highest point is **Montaña de la Caldera**, 127 m (417 ft) above sea level. It is home to over 130 species of plant and a variety of birdlife – but no seals. A circular walk around this beautiful and unspoilt island takes between three and four hours.

The whole area is a protected nature zone, so visitors need to obey certain rules: for example, keep to the marked paths; do not light fires outside the designated areas; do not leave or bury rubbish; do not remove any plants. To camp on the island you need to obtain authorisation from the Central Government (El Cabildo) of Fuerteventura, as you do if you want to gain access to the top of La Caldera.

Shopping

Although the seven Canary Islands are not very far apart, they each have something different to offer. Lanzarote is quite different from Fuerteventura in both its natural landscape and its shopping facilities.

Leaving Corralejo at 09.00 on Tuesdays, Thursdays and Saturdays, the ferry will arrive in Playa Blanca approximately 40 minutes later. A coach takes you to **Arrecife**, the modern capital of the Island, to spend two hours shopping and sampling street cafés. The coach then takes you to a small but modern shopping centre, **The Biosphere** in Puerto del Carmen,

⬥ *The stunning volcanic landscape of Lanzarote*

the hub of tourism on Lanzarote. Catch the ferry at 16.00, to arrive back at your hotel at about 17.00.

Timanfaya National Park

One learns about volcanoes in school, and of course they are seen from time to time on television, but, as with so many things, to experience their effects at first hand is an altogether different story. The sheer scale of the eruption, the solidified lava flow, the colours, the sulphurous smells and the heat so near the surface, all leave an impression.

Tours

César Manrique Tour The César Manrique Tour takes place on Fridays. Going straight from the ferry in Playa Blanca to the centre of the Island, where the Manrique monument dedicated to the farmers of Lanzarote stands, the tour will continue through the old capital of Teguise and stop for coffee at a viewpoint. Next on the itinerary is another viewpoint, **Mirador del Rio**, cleverly designed by the artist to blend into the cliffside. It offers spectacular vistas to the north. From here the coach descends to a choice of either the **Cueva de los Verdes** (Green Caves), which are natural and lead to an unexpected view, or **Jameos del Agua Caves** where you will be filled with wonder at how one man could transform an underground volcanic tube into an Aladdin's cave. There is a restaurant, a little natural seawater lake, dance floor, bars and an exotic palm-fringed swimming pool (now purely decorative). All this is landscaped, with curving steps, plants and water, complementing the colours and textures of the rocks.

On to **Punta de la Mujeres**, a sprawling fishing village and favourite summer resort for islanders, where there is a lunchtime stop.

The **Cactus Gardens** are the next port of call. These were the last creation of César Manrique before he died in a car accident in 1992. The highlight of this trip is a visit to the **Fundación César Manrique**, the artist's former home, which he designed in and above part of the lava flow. It is an incredible example of the skill of this man, who knew how to connect nature, life and art so successfully.

Lanzarote Grand Tour This tour takes place on Tuesdays, Thursdays and Saturdays. After the ferry crossing to Lanzarote, the Grand Tour starts with coffee in Yaiza, and continues to the **Timanfaya National Park**. This is followed by lunch, and a wine-tasting in the surrounding vineyards. The route then heads north, passing the **Monumento al Campesino** (Monument to the Countryman) created by César Manrique (see below) in the centre of the island. Next comes **Teguise**, the island's old capital, and up to the spectacular Famara cliffs, called **El Risco de Famara**. Here there is a short stop at the spectacular viewpoint overlooking much of the northern part of the island.

The tour continues through **Haría**, the valley of a thousand palm trees, and on to the famous volcanic caves, made so beautiful by César Manrique. You are then taken back along the east of the island to Playa Blanca for the return ferry trip across to Fuerteventura.

Lanzarote South Tour Scheduled for an early start on Mondays, Thursdays and Saturdays. After a 40-minute ferry trip to Lanzarote you arrive in **Playa Blanca**, the best planned and most rapidly developing tourist area. You head for coffee at **Yaiza**, one of Lanzarote's most attractive villages. Then it's on to an optional camel ride over a volcanic landscape, followed by a fascinating tour of **Timanfaya**, a protected National Park consisting of fields of lava, the result of an eruption lasting from 1730 to 1736. Evidence of the continuing ground heat will be dramatically demonstrated.

The next stop is for lunch amidst the island's wine-growing area, with an opportunity to sample some of the local wine. The last visit of the tour will be to **El Golfo**, a rugged coastal area with a unique green lagoon and the salt fields of El Janubio.

Returning to Fuerteventura, you will arrive back at your starting point at about 17.00.

 Windmills are a landmark in the countryside

LIFESTYLE
Island life

Food & drink

Canarians, like other Spaniards, love to eat out with friends and family, tucking into their food with a robust appetite, sharing noisy, convivial conversation, and letting children run and play around the table (there is no Spanish word for 'bedtime', and parents rarely go out without their children). Only the very smartest places demand any degree of formality. Apart from a light early breakfast of coffee and a pastry, meal times tend to be late by north European standards: about 14.00 for lunch and 21.00 for dinner. However, an exception is made for tourists. In the resorts, meals are served at all times of day. It is not unusual to see locals finishing lunch while tourists are beginning their evening meal. The standard of food on Fuerteventura is generally good, and it is reasonably priced.

INTERNATIONAL EATING

It would be perfectly possible to spend a fortnight on the island and eat nothing but Italian food, for example – and many holidaymakers do just that. With the local population so outnumbered by tourists, restaurants increasingly offer an international dining experience, with a variety of familiar home-from-home dishes like soups, steak and chips or omelettes. Paella and sangría are not local to Fuerteventura, coming from the Iberian peninsula, though both are to be found in the larger resorts. Needless to say, you will also find fish fingers and chips for children, along with Chinese and Indian cuisine, but we heartily recommend you try the local food.

GOFIO

For centuries *gofio* has been the staple food of the Canary Islands. It is relatively easy to make from toasted grains of maize, wheat or barley, ground into flour. The flour is kneaded with water and olive oil, sometimes with a little crumbled goat's cheese or honey added. The dough is then twisted into sticks and used as a type of bread.

It was easy for the island's goatherds or fishermen, who were often away for days at a time, to take these sticks of *gofio* with them as staple

🔺 Papas arrugadas con mojo – *crispy potatoes with piquant sauce*

provisions; it rarely went off and was very sustaining. Breakfast today, for many locals, often still consists of milky coffee with *gofio*.

Local soups and stews – for example *potaje*, *puchero* and *sancocho* (see page 89) – are thickened with *gofio* flour, making them more substantial.

MOJO

The most uniquely Canarian phrase on the menu is *con mojo*, 'with *mojo*'. Grilled or fried fish, roasted meats or boiled vegetables, almost anything may be served *con mojo*. *Mojo* (pronounced *mo-ho*) is the piquant sauce of the Canary Islands. Based on olive oil, it comes in different versions, and in good restaurants is more or less spicy according to what it accompanies. *Mojo* comes in two colours – red and green. Coriander and parsley make *mojo verde* (green *mojo*), which has a refreshing bite, while hot chillis are used in the spicier *mojo rojo* (red *mojo*).

TAPAS

This is good way to try out a variety of local dishes. Tapas are small portions of food (*tapa* means lid or small dish), often served as a side dish. The problem can be in knowing what to ask for. Normally there is a good selection of tapas on display in either chilled or heated cabinets on the bar. If you want a portion, ask for *una ración* (pronounced *rass-ee-on*).

GOAT'S CHEESE

Mojo is the perfect accompaniment for fried or grilled goat's cheese (*queso de cabra*), served as a delicious starter. Cheese has an important part in the local diet, and is often eaten as tapas or just with a glass of wine. *Majorero* is a traditional Fuerteventuran speciality and a gourmet's delight, acclaimed throughout Spain. It is made with goat's milk and has a dense texture and strong but smooth flavour. Older *majorero* can be coated with oil and paprika or *gofio*. The local goat's cheese is delicious and is categorised as follows:

Fresco – a fresh, soft and moist white cheese.

Semi-curado – left to mature for a month and is of a firmer texture.

Curado – after two months it begins to dry, becoming a harder cheese.

Viejo – at least six months old, by which time it is almost as hard as Parmesan, which it resembles.

MEAT

Wild game and pork are the favourites on the island. Goats are ubiquitous, you'll see them everywhere you go, either in herds or tethered singly. They are hardy, easy to look after, and are traditionally one of the island's main sources of meat. Goat is usually served roasted (*al horno*) or in a stew. Rabbits were introduced by the first settlers and they bred well and became a staple source of fresh meat. Fuerteventura's rabbit population was not subjected to the ravages of myxomatosis, and they are very plentiful. Rabbit dishes continue to be popular today. Pigs are kept on the island, although to a much lesser extent than goats, and island-bred pork is full of flavour. As most livestock in Fuerteventura is brought up in a state of semi-freedom, their meat is of high quality.

Puchero is a classic Canarian stew, thick and savoury, made with lentils, chickpeas, vegetables and two or more kinds of meat, including pork.

⬤ *A goat farm in the mountains*

CHURROS

A firm batter is formed into long-sausage-like shapes and then deep-fried, not unlike traditional fairground doughnuts. Traditionally *churros* are dipped in a thick chocolate drink (*churros con chocolate*) or in coffee.

FISH

Since most of the coastal resorts were formerly fishing ports, it is not surprising that fish is an island staple. More unexpected is that on Fuerteventura traditionally fish is salted and preserved instead of being eaten fresh. Because of seasonal food shortages in the past, various kinds of plentiful fish were preserved when caught – gutted as soon as possible and hung up in the sun until dry. This practice continues today. Another way of preservation is to salt the fish, which is then used to make a dish called *sancocho*, still a traditional island favourite. *Sancocho* is a fish stew made with potatoes and vegetables.

FRUIT & VEGETABLES

These are very fresh, in spite of the fact that the majority come from other Canarian islands or mainland Spain. Potatoes are a staple – a typical local dish is *papas arrugadas* (locally grown, very wrinkly potatoes cooked in their skins with a salty crust). These are especially good eaten with either *mojo verde* or *mojo rojo*.

DESSERTS

Canarios have a sweet tooth, and may finish a meal with the islanders' traditional dessert, *bienmesabe*, a syrupy, nutty concoction, often served with ice cream. *Gofio* desserts are rather stodgy and syrupy, but *flan gofio* or *frangollo*, flavoured with lemon, is quite delicious. All restaurants have their home specialities, which are well worth trying.

WINE

Unlike its neighbour, Lanzarote, Fuerteventura produces very little wine. The wine from Tefia is the most interesting, for a table wine.

Menu decoder

SNACKS/SIDE ORDERS/TAPAS
Aceitunas con mojo Olives with hot sauce
Bocadillo (pronounced *bocadee-yo*) Filled roll
Chipirones Small squid
Ensalada Salad
Gambas ajillo Garlic prawns
Perrito caliente Hot-dog
Queso Cheese
Tapas Snacks

STARTERS
Potaje Thick soup of vegetables and pulses – may contain added meat
Potaje de berros Watercress soup

MAIN COURSES
Cabrito Kid (goat)
Caldo de pescado Fish, vegetables and maize meal stew
Conejo al salmorejo Rabbit marinated in hot chilli sauce
Garbanzada Chickpea stew with meat
Lomo Slices of cured pork

Pata de cerdo Roast leg of pork
Pechuga empanada Breaded chicken breast or chicken breast in batter
Puchero Meat and vegetable stew
Ranchos Noodles, beef and chickpeas
Ropa vieja Chickpeas, vegetables and potatoes (although meat can be added)
Sancocho Salted fish (often *cherne*, a kind of sea bass) with potatoes and sweet potatoes

DESSERTS
Arroz con leche Cold rice pudding with cinnamon
Bienmesabe A mix of honey and almonds (delicious poured over ice cream)
Flan Crème caramel
Fruta del tiempo Fresh fruit in season
Helado Ice cream
Truchas Turnovers filled with pumpkin or sweet potato

DRINKS

Agua (pronounced *ah-whah*)
    mineral Mineral water
    con gas/sin gas Fizzy/still
Batido Milkshake
Café Coffee
    con leche Made with milk
    cortado Small white coffee
    descafeinado
    Decaffeinated
    solo Black
Carajillo Coffee with a bit of
    condensed milk and a drop
    of alcohol
Cerveza Beer
Leche Milk
Limonada Lemonade
Naranja Orange
Ron Local rum
Té Tea
Vino Wine
    blanco White
    rosado Rosé
    tinto Red

SPECIALITY DRINKS

Bitter kas Similar to Campari
    but non-alcoholic
Cocktail Atlántico Rum, dry
    gin, banana liqueur, blue
    curaçao, pineapple juice
Cocktail Canario Rum, banana
    cream liqueur, orange juice,
    cointreau, a drop of
    grenadine
Guindilla Rum-based cherry
    liqueur
Mora Blackberry liqueur
Ron miel Rum with honey,
    a local speciality
Sangria Mix of red wine,
    spirits and fruit juices; can
    be made with champagne
    on request

Shopping

Although part of the EU, the Canary Islands have a special duty-free status. Therefore they are treated as a non-EU region for allowances. You will probably find it is very tempting to spend a lot on duty-free goods – the prices are often lower than in the UK. But be warned – when you return home, there is a limit to the value of goods you are allowed to bring in without attracting tax. These allowances vary, and they do apply to tobacco, alcohol and perfume. Check with your travel agent before you leave.

It is difficult to be specific about shop opening hours. Local shops typically open from 09.00–13.00 and 16.30–19.30 or 20.00 in the week (almost everything shuts down for *siesta* in the afternoon). On Saturdays, local shops usually close for the day at 13.00. In tourist centres they tend to open from 10.00–22.00 (supermarkets 08.30–21.00).

All resorts have shopping centres with good supermarkets. There are some colourful open-air markets in various tourist areas, starting early and finishing at about 13.00.

You can expect to bargain at markets, and at many of the duty-free shops in tourist resorts. When making a large purchase, be sure that you get a proper money-back guarantee, and if appropriate that an international warranty is included and properly completed. Beware

MARKETS
Most island communities have open-air markets. You will find a huge selection of things to buy and it is fun to haggle. Most take place in the morning.
Caleta de Fuste Saturday – Castillo Plaza
Corralejo Monday and Friday – Baku Complex, on the main road to La Oliva
Costa Calma Sunday – on the main road north of town
Morro Jable Thursday – Avenida Saladar

of scams, and be sure to check all receipts before paying, including those from restaurants. Beware also of counterfeit goods, and treat any bargain-priced electrical goods and cameras as suspect. Souvenir shops are everywhere, but their goods, apart from local crafts, are not necessarily made in Fuerteventura.

◔ You'll find multicoloured woven bags and baskets on sale in the markets

TRADITIONAL CRAFTS

Openwork embroidery This is one of the oldest traditional crafts in the Canary Islands, dating back to the days of the early settlers. You will see traycloths, table runners and mats, aprons, handkerchiefs and little dolls. It is possible to see women at work at many of the island's craft centres.

Weaving Again, this dates back to the days of the early settlers. You will find handwoven bags, material for costumes worn by the folklore groups, blankets and rugs.

Basketwork This is a really functional part of the local handicrafts, the raw material being palm leaves which are found in abundance. Originally there was a large demand for basketwork for domestic and personal use. Nowadays, basketwork is almost exclusively ornamental.

Green palm leaves are made into saddle bags, mats, brooms and grain storage baskets. Strips of green palm leaf are woven for moulding cheese, and white palm leaves are made into hats, baskets and fans.

Pottery The ancient inhabitants of the island, the 'Majos', introduced the making of earthenware pottery from the north of Africa. Aboriginal pottery was shaped by hand and was typically oval with a conical or flat bottom, the surface being decorated with dots or slashes. When the island was colonised this typical design was abandoned and different shapes, sizes and modes of decoration were adopted.

The robust pottery is still made by hand without using a wheel or moulds. The most common artefacts are cooking pots, baking dishes, milk jars and fertility symbols.

The *zurrón* This is a bag made from the skin of a goat kid. It is used to knead *gofio* (see pages 84–5). The *zurrón* is one of the most common artefacts found throughout the island history.

Olivina Olivina is a Canarian volcanic, green, semi-precious stone that is made into jewellery, which you will find for sale at reasonable prices.

Children

Fuerteventura is a very child-friendly place where families are made welcome in restaurants, bars or entertainments. The tolerant attitude towards children ensures that they too will have a good holiday. Off the beach there are enough activities to keep them happily occupied.

You will find that nearly all villages have a designated playground area with swings, slides and other amusements. These are usually close to the centre and well constructed. Locals will go out of their way to pander to the young – in a busy Canarian bar, if a child struggles up onto a stool and asks for a glass of water, he or she will be served immediately!

Fuerteventura, with its sandy beaches, is a paradise for young children. A top favourite activity for both children and adults is rolling down the sand dunes near Corralejo, where the dunes rise to heights of 10 m (30 ft) or more. Paddling is great, with no worrying about treading on rocks, but children will need strict supervision, as the sea around Fuerteventura can be rough. As there is so often a breeze, kite-flying is great fun.

ACTIVITIES FOR CHILDREN

There are many boating and diving activities available at all the resorts, but many only cater for children over 12 years old. Baku, in Corralejo (see page 17), however, has facilities for all children, young and old. Tennis, riding, go-karting and camel rides are within easy reach of most tourist centres (see individual Resorts, pages 13–52), and many of the excursions (see pages 53–82) are also suitable for families. Other places of special interest for children are the aquarium in Tarajalejo (see page 96) and the zoo park in La Lajita (see below). The *Pedra Sartaña* pirate-style ship that sails from Morro Jable harbour is also a great choice. ☎ 670 745 191 🌐 www.excursiones-barco-fuerteventura.com 🕐 Sails Mon–Sat

La Lajita Oasis Park

Set amidst lush tropical gardens in the Oasis Park in the village of La Lajita (see page 73), this small zoo park is home to a wide variety of

▲ *Splashy fun at the sea lion show at La Lajita Oasis Park*

> ### STAY SAFE IN THE SUN
> Be careful of the strength of the sun in Fuerteventura. When it is windy, the temperature can seem deceptively cool. A high-factor sunblock is a must and it is sensible for children to wear a hat, preferably one with elastic under the chin to stop it being blown away!

birds, reptiles, primates and other mammals. Twice daily there are parrot shows, but the highlight for children is the 30-minute camel safari. Treks take place throughout the day according to demand. Ponies and donkeys are also available for rides, and feeding of the crocodiles takes place around once a week. There are also play areas, a bar and restaurant and also a souvenir shop. ❶ 928 343 047 ❷ 09.30–18.00 daily ❶ Admission charge

El Centro de Ocio El Brasero
There is an aquarium just outside the village of Tarajalejo (see page 72), which has three large tanks of Canarian fish. ❸ Carretera General Tarajalejo ❶ 928 161 182 ❷ Tues–Sun 10.00–20.00; closed Mon

Carnival
This is a dazzling show that takes place all over the island (see page 103). Much of the spectacle revolves around the crowning of the Carnival Queen. The funfairs (which don't usually get going until around 19.00) are great for the children, and they will also enjoy the noise, colour and flamboyance of the parade.

The Dia de Reyes parade (6 January – see page 104) is also a magic event for children, who can get to tell their wishes to the *Reyes Magos* (the Wise Men).

Sports & activities

Fuerteventura is an ideal place for activities on both land and water. Walking, riding and cycling are readily available, and the hiking is superb – there's something for all levels of fitness and there are no real restrictions on walking wherever you want. The tourist offices have leaflets suggesting good routes. The snorkelling is wonderful and the scuba diving even better.

SUGGESTED WALKING & HIKING ROUTES

None of the routes described below is difficult, and they are designed to take no more than half a day to accomplish. They will all give you wonderful views. When walking, be mindful of crops, do not damage walls you may have to cross, or disturb the domesticated animals. Make sure you wear proper shoes, and remember to take a hat, sunblock and plenty of water. It is a wise precaution to let someone know where you plan to go.

Tuineje–Toto

Set off from Tuineje, go past the cemetery and continue until you reach the top of Mount Manitaga, where you will enjoy magnificent views over the whole island. Go down along the road towards Toto. Examples of the native flora and fauna can be seen along this route.
Estimated time Between 3 and 4 hours
Degree of difficulty Average

Tiscamanita–Pozo Negro

Leave Tiscamanita and go along the ravine, through an aloe vera plantation, until you reach the Caldera de la Laguna de las Mujeres. After you have crossed the Malpaís Grande, you will reach Pozo Negro.
Estimated time Between 3 and 4 hours
Degree of difficulty Average

Lajares–Corralejo

From Lajares take the path to the Calderón Hondo volcanoes. Follow the Majanicho road, which will take you into the volcanic area known as

● *Kite-surfers on Flag Beach near Corralejo*

Mascona. There are wonderful views towards Lajares and the southern part of the island along this stretch of the route. Calderón Hondo is a circular volcanic cone that is around 70 m (230 ft) deep. The Caldera Encantada is well worth visiting, before continuing through the Morro del Fraile to Corralejo.

Estimated time Between 3 and 4 hours
Degree of difficulty Average

El Malpaís de la Arena

Located in the north of the island, this route starts close to Villaverde. The stretch from the Montaña del Molino to the Montaña de los Saltos runs beside the walls that separate El Malpaís de la Arena from the farming land around Villaverde. From La Hoya del Agua, you will get a beautiful view over the northern part of Fuerteventura. The old lava flows from the Villaverde volcanoes and those that make up El Malpaís de la Arena can be seen clearly. From the base of the Montaña de la Arena you can look across and see the Isla de los Lobos and Lanzarote.

Estimated time Between 3 and 4 hours
Degree of difficulty Average

Barranco de la Herradura

The route starts from just outside Puerto del Rosario, at the mouth of the ravine that runs to Time. As you progress along this route, you will be able to see the ruins of early settlements, and local flora and fauna.

Estimated time 3 hours
Degree of difficulty Easy

Barranco de los Molinos

Located 4 km (2½ miles) from Tefía, the Barranco is a deep and wide ravine that runs down into the sea, and is home to many of the island's native plants.

Estimated time Between 2 and 3 hours
Degree of difficulty Easy

Barranco de Butihondo–Pico de la Zarza

Located in the southern part of the island, this is a small route along the Barranco de Butihondo which will take you to the top of the highest point of the island, at 807 m (2,648 ft). From the peak, on a clear day you will be able to see some of the islands to the west.

Estimated time Approximately 3 hours
Degree of difficulty Average

Cañada del Rio–La Pared

This walk is in the southwest of the island. It is a fascinating route through the Island's most desert-like region, where you will get magnificent views over the enormous El Jable dunes, the amazing coastline and the wild and turbulent Atlantic.

Estimated time Approximately 3 hours
Degree of difficulty Easy

Barranco de la Vega–Malpaso

Located in the centre of the island, this route follows the path of the *barranco*, a large ravine, past a tiny dam and down through some surprising mountains, where you can visit a delightful chapel said to be the site of an appearance by Our Lady of La Peña.

Estimated time Approximately 2 hours
Degree of difficulty Easy

Caleta de Fuste–Salinas del Carmen

This walk was part of the road that joined Puerto del Rosario and Antigua. The route starts from the beach at Caleta de Fuste, and is an opportunity to visit Caleta's fortified castle. Walk south along the shore of the beach and past the lime kilns at La Guirra. The destination is the only working salt mine left on the island. There is a tiny fishing village in the area, where you can either stop at the beach or continue south to the ravine known as the Barranco de la Torre.

Estimated time Approximately 3 hours
Degree of difficulty Easy

⬥ *Fuerteventuran waters are great for windsurfing*

WILDLIFE WATCHING

Because Fuerteventura is a desert-like island, wildlife has to struggle harder in order to survive. Two of the island's endangered species are the Egyptian vulture and the Houbara bustard, both of which are protected. The Houbara bustard is at last making good progress and breeding well. However, the Egyptian vulture is still struggling to increase its numbers, partly due to the changing environment in Fuerteventura over the years, and the fact that the young birds do not become sexually active until they are five or six years old.

Rabbits do well here, vying with the goats for food. The chipmunks or ground squirrels, although not a native species (they were originally brought from North Africa), increase each year. Perhaps most strangely, the island supports a population of hedgehogs.

Under the water the bays and rock pools teem with varied and colourful specimens. Snorkelling is an absolute delight, not only for seeing the fish, but for the profusion of plant life. Scuba diving is even better. Sometimes, if you are really lucky, you might see whales, dolphins and turtles.

WINDSURFING & KITEBOARDING

Just south of Costa Calma on **Playa de Sotavento**, the PWA/ISA Windsurfing World Cup Championship is held every year at the end of July, followed immediately by the World Kiteboarding Grand Prix. These spectacular competitions attract the best boarders in the world, competing for thousands of euros in prize money. The area is known for its strong, gusty offshore winds, which can reach up to 50 knots (almost 100 km/h), so you can be sure to see some breathtaking moments, and will be able to admire the great bravery and skill of the participants. The temptation to emulate the contestants is strong, and the southern part of the island always attracts a large number of surfing fans.

Festivals & events

Festivals, or fiestas, are an integral part of Canarian life. They are partly religious, with recreational and cultural activities taking place at the same time. The whole community joins in, either with the preparations or just by being there. The exuberance is infectious.

Island fiestas are characterised by colourful processions, sometimes complete with donkey carts laden with sustenance for the forthcoming hours – and also available for both children and the elderly to hitch a ride when in need of a rest. The celebrations are accompanied by masses of eating and drinking, dancing and folk music.

Age-old games are played, sometimes with competitions between nearby villages. Stalls have a fairground feel about them, offering sweets and amusements for children and alcoholic pick-me-ups for the adults. In the evening there are concerts, plays and dancing, with rock groups hired for the younger generation. In some of the more isolated villages, you can still see black-clad grandmas or maiden aunts sitting on benches around the dance floor, following the old chaperone rules! All these activities go on well into the early hours. The bigger fiestas often finish with spectacular displays of fireworks. Most individual villages have their own fiesta day, so look out for bunting in the streets and ask when the 'big day' is. On the main fiesta days, and away from the main tourist areas, neither shops nor banks will be open. Most main-road petrol stations, however, have a self-service credit card system, but try not to rely on this.

CARNIVAL

Almost every village, town and city hosts its own carnival between January and April every year. The date the festival takes place varies as it depends when Easter falls. Carnival, which often lasts for nine or ten days, is a time to let your hair down and join in with the fun. Many of the floats and groups are imaginatively and elaborately decorated, having taken the whole year to prepare.

The festivities usually start around 17.00, and go on for several hours, depending on the number of floats. The local people tend to make this event an all-night affair with much drinking. Visitors are always welcome to join in, and you will find yourself totally caught up in the exhilarating atmosphere, infected by the beat of the various bands as they pass. Local shops often sell inexpensive, ready-made costumes, if you don't fancy putting something together for yourself. During Carnival there are excellent professional shows and concerts, most of which are free of charge and open to the public, plus funfairs for the children.

DÍA DE REYES

This is the first major festival of the year. The Holy Day of the Three Kings takes place on 6 January in Corralejo and the capital, Puerto del Rosario. It is a wonderful occasion during which the three 'kings' parade through the town riding camels, accepting letters from children (similar to the letters that children in Britain send to Father Christmas) and distributing

⬤ *A sand sculpture on the beach celebrates New Year*

FESTIVALS & NATIONAL HOLIDAYS

1 January	New Year
6 January	Día de Reyes
January–April	Carnival – events all over the island. Dates vary in each village according to when Easter falls
March/April	Easter – events all over the island
March/April	El Entierro de la Sardina – Ash Wednesday
1 May	Labour Day
30 May	Canary Island Autonomy Day
15 August	The Assumption of the Virgin Mary
September	Fiesta de Nuestra Señora de la Peña
12 October	Spain's National Day
1 November	All Saints' Day
6 December	Constitution Day
8 December	The Immaculate Conception
25 December	Christmas Day

sweets to the spellbound wide-eyed youngsters, who wait below with outstretched hands. Most of the small villages also celebrate this fiesta in some way.

EL ENTIERRO DE LA SARDINA

Translated as 'The Burial of the Sardine', this ancient custom started in the mists of time, as a pagan celebration, to symbolise the purging of the bad things that happened during the previous year, and to start afresh. It takes place across the island on Ash Wednesday. The form it takes now is most unusual, with an enormous, beautifully crafted sardine carried on a bier and followed by wailing mourners (men dressed in black as widows). The sardine is carried to the beach, and is not in fact buried, but instead is burnt in a huge fire. This celebration marks the end of Carnival.

FIESTA DE NUESTRA SEÑORA DE LA PEÑA

Fuerteventura's predominant religious festival takes place on the third Saturday in September in **Vega del Río Palmas**, when the rediscovered statue of the Virgen de la Peña is paraded with much solemnity on a litter, carried on the shoulders of selected men. Around the feet of the statue in great profusion are decorations of flowers and candles.

A *romería* is a pilgrimage, and people from all corners of the island, dressed in local costume, make their way to Vega, singing Canarian folk music accompanied by musicians playing instruments such as the timple, bandurrias, laud, mandolin, guitar and violin. There are pauses for traditional dancing (the most famous of which is the polka, originally brought over from Poland), eating and drinking. Home-made food is dispensed to the spectators from hand-woven bags or baskets, and home-brewed drink from leather bottles called *botas*. The women wear enormous hats, not unlike Mexican sombreros (these are made locally from young, bleached palm leaves), and huge black shawls which they prop up on the points of their hats to create a larger degree of shade.

▶ *Cycling the coastal roads of Fuerteventura*

PRACTICAL INFORMATION
Tips & advice

Accommodation

Price ratings are based on a double room for one night.
£ up to €100   **££** €100–150   **£££** over €150

CORRALEJO
Hotel Arena £ A great value 4-star hotel with 101 rooms, a buffet restaurant and a swimming pool with poolside bar. ⓐ Calle El Moro ⓣ 928 536 034 ⓦ www.hotelarenacorralejo.com

BlueBay Palace ££ This award-winning hotel is ideally located near the beach, restaurants and shops. The facilities are of a high standard with excellent service and a friendly atmosphere. ⓐ Avenida Grandes Playas 12 ⓣ 928 536 050 ⓦ www.bluebayresorts.com

Gran Hotel Atlantis Bahía Real £££ A fantastic all-round 5-star hotel offering swimming pools, five restaurants, two bars, exercise classes, bus to beach service, hydrotherapy and other pampering services. You certainly get what you pay for! ⓐ Avenida Grandes Playas ⓣ 928 536 444 ⓦ www.atlantishotels.com

PUERTO DEL ROSARIO
Hotel JM ££ A comfortable and convenient hotel, located on the seafront. It has an excellent cafeteria with buffet breakfast, plus accommodation suitable for travellers with disabilities. ⓐ Avenida Marítima 9 ⓣ 928 859 464 ⓦ www.jmhotelpuertodelrosario.com

Hotel Playa Blanca ££ This elegant old hotel was formerly a parador. Located right beside a pretty beach, the rooms are charming with wonderful views. ⓐ Playa Blanca 45 ⓣ 928 851 150

CALETA DE FUSTE
Beach Club Hotel £ At just 2 km (1 mile) from the beach, this 2-star hotel has a great pool and some lovely gardens to stroll around. Hotel guests

are permitted to make full use of the hotel's nearby sister resort, Club Montecastillo. ⓐ Calle San Francisco ☏ 928 163 620

Hotel Elba Sara ££–£££ One of the island's more upmarket hotels, this 4-star 266-bedroom luxury hotel also has a great restaurant with terrace. ⓐ Golf Resort, Calle Jandía, Km 11 ☏ 928 160 020 Ⓦ www.hoteles elba.com ⓔ elbasara@hoteleselba.com

COSTA CALMA
Sunrise Monica Beach Hotel ££ Located very near the beach, this 3-star hotel has plenty of sports, leisure and entertainment facilities, 410 rooms, a restaurant and shopping. ⓐ Avenida Jahn Reisen ☏ 928 547 214

Hotel Rio Calma £££ A 4-star hotel, also located near the beach, it has 384 rooms and is six storeys high. There are facilities for childcare, all sorts of pampering treats and a restaurant serving international cuisine. ⓐ Calle Artistas Canarios 8 ☏ 928 546 050

JANDÍA PLAYA
Barceló Jandía Playa ££–£££ Right by Jandía beach and very near Morro Jable, this large hotel doesn't do things by halves: it has a poolside snack bar, five bars, two restaurants and a disco. There are also four swimming pools, solarium, whirlpool, childcare facilities and a theatre hall. ⓐ Calle La Mancha, Barranco de Vinamar ☏ 928 547 517 Ⓦ www.barcelo.com

Hotel Riu Palace Jandía ££–£££ Also by Jandía beach, very near Morro Jable, this 4-star hotel's location is perfect for watersports enthusiasts. There are 209 en-suite rooms, a cocktail bar, restaurant, lounge and whirlpool. ⓐ Playa Jandía ☏ 928 540 370 Ⓦ www.riu.com

MORRO JABLE
Faro Jandia ££ Excellent facilities, spacious rooms and attractive architecture make this a great choice. ⓐ Avenida del Saladar 17 ☏ 928 545 035 Ⓦ www.hotel-farojandia.com

Preparing to go

GETTING THERE

By far the easiest and least expensive way to visit Fuerteventura is on a package holiday. Inclusive packages, operated by all the major travel companies, leave from all over northern Europe several times weekly. You will find tour operators featuring Fuerteventura at ⓦ www.abta.com

For travellers who already have accommodation in Fuerteventura, or wish to book hotels directly, both charter and scheduled airlines sell low-cost direct flights to the island from London and most UK regional airports. Flights from the US go to Puerto del Rosario via Madrid, Spain.

Other search engines for cheap scheduled and charter flights include:
ⓦ www.lastminute.com
ⓦ www.flightline.co.uk
ⓦ www.skyscanner.net

The following companies offer flights to Fuerteventura:
easyJet (ⓦ www.easyjet.com): from Liverpool and Stansted.
flythomascook (ⓦ http://book.flythomascook.com): from East Midlands, Gatwick, Glasgow International, Humberside, Leeds, Luton, Manchester, Newcastle and Stansted.
Thomsonfly (ⓦ www.thomsonfly.com): from Newcastle, Manchester, Stansted, Gatwick, Glasgow International, East Midlands, Cardiff, Bristol and Birmingham.

Many people are aware that air travel emits CO_2, which contributes to climate change. You may be interested in the possibility of lessening the environmental impact of your flight through the charity **Climate Care**, which offsets your CO_2 by funding environmental projects around the world. Visit ⓦ www.climatecare.org

TOURISM AUTHORITY

Spanish Tourist Office ⓐ UK office: 79 New Cavendish St, London W1W 6XB ⓘ 020 7486 8077 ⓕ 020 7486 8034 ⓦ www.spain.info ⓛ 09.15–16.15

Mon–Fri; visits by appointment only ➋ Republic of Ireland office: PO Box 10015, Dublin 1 🕐 09.15–16.15 Mon–Fri
24-hour brochure request line ☎ UK: 08459 400 180 ☎ Republic of Ireland: 0818 220 290 ❶ Calls are charged at national rates

BEFORE YOU LEAVE

All EU and US citizens are free to travel to Fuerteventura. No inocula-
tions or health preparations are needed. It is a good idea to pack a small
first-aid kit to carry with you containing plasters, antiseptic cream,
travel-sickness pills, insect repellent and/or bite-relief cream,
antihistamine tablets, upset stomach remedies and painkillers. You
might want to bring a selection of sunblock and high-factor lotions if
you have children with you, and don't forget after-sun cream as well.
If you are taking prescription medicines, ensure that you take enough
for the duration of your visit, and an extra copy of the information
sheet in case of loss, but you may find it impossible to obtain the same
medicines in Fuerteventura. It is also worth having a dental check-up
before you go.

ENTRY FORMALITIES

The most important documents you will need are your tickets and
your passport. Check well in advance that your passport is up to date
and has at least three months left to run (six months is even better).
All children, including newborn babies, need their own passport.
It generally takes at least three weeks to process a passport renewal.
This can be longer in the run-up to the summer months. Contact the
Identity and Passport Service for the latest information on how to renew
your passport and the processing times involved. ☎ 0300 222 0000
🌐 www.direct.gov.uk

If you are thinking of hiring a car while you are away, you will need to
have your UK driving licence with you. If you want more than one driver
for the car, the other drivers must have their licences too. Make sure to
bring both parts of the licence.

INSURANCE

All UK residents are entitled to reduced cost or free medical treatment when temporarily visiting any country within the European Union (EU), including Spain. To obtain this treatment you will need to get a European Health Insurance Card (EHIC), which is free of charge. The government stresses that the European Health Insurance Card should not be a replacement for travel insurance and it is highly recommended that travellers cover themselves for unexpected costs, including medical emergency repatriation, and the loss of, or damage, to any belongings. For more information, see Ⓦ www.dh.gov.uk/travellers

MONEY

The currency in the Canaries is the same as in mainland Spain: the euro, with one euro broken down into 100 cents or *céntimos*. Notes come in denominations of €5, €10, €20, €50, €100, €200 and €500. Coins are available in denominations of €1, €2 and 1, 2, 5, 10, 20 and 50 cents. You will need some currency before you go, especially if your flight gets you to your destination at the weekend or late in the day after the banks have closed. You can exchange money at the airport before you depart. You should also make sure that your credit, charge and debit cards are up to date – you do not want them to expire mid-holiday – and that your credit limit is sufficient to allow you to make those holiday purchases. Once you arrive, you will find cash dispensers in all the resorts.

CLIMATE

The climate is moderately steady throughout the year, with temperatures ranging from about 14°C to 27°C (57°F to 81°F) and with plenty of sunshine all the year round. Almost all the rain falls in the winter, but even in the wettest months (December/January) rainfall totals average only 2.7 cm (just over 1 in) per month. However, it can be chilly in the evenings during the winter months, so it is advisable to take something warmer for the evenings.

Be sure that young children wear something on their heads, because the UV rays are strong and there is often a strong breeze on the island that makes you less conscious of how hot the sun is.

BAGGAGE ALLOWANCE

Baggage allowances vary according to the airline, destination and class of travel, but 15–20 kg (33–44 lb) per person is the norm for luggage that is carried in the hold (it usually tells you what the weight limit is on your ticket). You are also allowed one item of cabin baggage usually weighing no more than 5 kg (11 lb), though some airlines allow 10 kg (22 lb), measuring a maximum of 46 by 30 by 23 cm (18 by 12 by 9 in). Rules for package-tour charter flights may be different, so it is always important to enquire in advance.

In addition, you can usually carry your duty-free purchases, umbrella, coat, camera, etc. as hand baggage. Large items – surfboards, golf clubs, collapsible wheelchairs and pushchairs – are usually charged as extras and it is a good idea to let the airline know in advance if you want to bring these.

During your stay

AIRPORTS

The international airport in Fuerteventura is a modern and impressive building. It is situated very close to the capital, Puerto del Rosario, and only ten minutes by car from the resort of Caleta de Fuste. Flights mainly arrive from Europe and other Canary islands, with over four million passengers passing through every year. You can get to and from the airport by taxi, which can be found directly outside Arrivals, or by coach transfer if travelling on a package tour. There are also two bus routes serving the airport. The main Fuerteventura airport bus leaves every 30 minutes and runs between Puerto del Rosario and Caleta de Fuste. The second airport bus is not as frequent and runs between the capital and Morro Jable, in the south of the island.

COMMUNICATIONS

If you wish to use your mobile phone on holiday, check with your operator before you leave to find out how much the calls will cost you.

Phone booths in Fuerteventura take credit cards or phone cards, which can be purchased in post offices and supermarkets.

The postal service in Spain is called *correos*. You'll find large branches in the major towns, which generally open all day Monday to Saturday. Smaller branches in outlying towns and villages may only be open in the morning. Post boxes in Fuerteventura are bright yellow.

While Internet access is becoming more common in larger hotels, do not assume that public Internet points will be readily available throughout the island. Ask at your hotel or at the tourist office for the nearest one.

CUSTOMS

As a rule the people of Fuerteventura follow many of the same day-to-day customs as people in the rest of Spain, especially in terms of how they relate to one another. Generally they are sociable and are likely to greet and say goodbye to strangers in public places. When they are

⬥ *Puerto del Rosario harbour*

TELEPHONING FUERTEVENTURA

Fuerteventura is part of Spain. Dial 34 for Spain, followed by 928, which is the Fuerteventura area code, followed by the six-digit number.

TELEPHONING ABROAD

The dialling code for international access is 00. Follow this by the country code (UK **44**, US and Canada **1**, Australia **61**, New Zealand **64**, South Africa **27**, Republic of Ireland **353**) and then the area code minus the initial 0. The cheapest time to call home is after 20.00 on Saturday and all day Sunday.

introduced they shake hands, and women will kiss one another on each cheek. Close friends and family members often kiss when they meet and say goodbye. People also often follow quite a rigid order to their day, starting work early, taking a long lunch and often a siesta, followed by a return to work or meeting friends for tea or an early evening drink. Dinner will invariably be late. It's always a good idea to try to adapt to the local traditions and rhythms of the day, as you will get more out of your stay.

DRESS CODES

The islanders are Catholic, so it is respectful to them not to go into churches (or even the bigger towns such as Puerto del Rosario) wearing skimpy shorts and tops, or shirtless. Of course, beachwear is absolutely fine for the holiday resorts.

ELECTRICITY

The islands have the same voltage as the UK, but with two-pin plugs, so you will need to bring an adaptor. These are readily available in the UK at electrical shops or major chemists. If you are considering buying electrical appliances to take home, always check that they will work in the UK before you buy.

EMERGENCIES

The **British Consulate Las Palmas** on Gran Canaria is the nearest British consul. **ⓐ** Consular Section, Calle Luis Morote 6 – 3rd floor, Las Palmas de Gran Canaria, Canary Islands **ⓣ** 902 109 356/913 342 194 **ⓕ** 928 267 774 **ⓔ** LasPalmas.Consulate@fco.gov.uk **ⓦ** http://ukinspain.fco.gov.uk/en

GETTING AROUND
Car hire & driving

The police are very kind, understanding and helpful, but they are very firm, so do uphold the law. As in the UK, drinking and driving is severely dealt with. The driver and all passengers must wear a seat belt. Children under ten must travel in the back of the car. If your car uses unleaded petrol, you need *gasolina sin plomo*.

Car hire in Spain and its islands has become increasingly competitive. Before you go check out the various price-comparison websites for the best deals. Once on the island, shop around the local companies – even in high season you'll find they are in serious competition with each

EMERGENCY NUMBERS
General emergency and ambulance **ⓣ** 112
Police **ⓣ** 091
Fire Brigade **ⓣ** 080
Guardia Civil emergency number **ⓣ** 062

Guardia Civil local numbers:
Puerto del Rosario **ⓣ** 928 851 100
Morro Jable **ⓣ** 928 541 107
Gran Tarajal **ⓣ** 928 870 031

National Police:
Puerto del Rosario **ⓣ** 928 850 909

Puerto del Rosario General Hospital **ⓣ** 928 531 799

other. Some companies will take a deposit to cover any insurance excess if the car is damaged. Some will also charge you for a tank of petrol, while others will not charge you for fuel, but will expect the car to be returned full. When collecting the car you will need to present both parts of your driving licence and a valid credit card, usually the one you booked the car with.

Rules of the road Remember to drive on the right. Never cross a solid line when on a slip road joining a main road – make sure you wait until you get to the dotted line part before filtering in. Remember to give way to traffic coming from your left when you are on a roundabout, and to go round it anticlockwise. Motorists must carry their driving licences, passports and car-hire documents at all times. Failure to do so will result in an automatic on-the-spot fine if you are stopped in one of the frequent road checks.

Roads In general, the road surfaces are good. Road markings are clear, but some of the traffic systems can be confusing when first encountered. Be aware that traffic priorities in these complex traffic systems do not always conform to your expectations: you might find a stop sign part-way around a roundabout or even on a motorway.

Petrol This is inexpensive on the islands and petrol stations are frequent along main routes. Always fill up with petrol before heading off into the hills or the interior.

Parking Parking meters are usual in built-up or popular areas. Here the parking spaces are marked out in blue. Pay at the meter and display

SPEED LIMITS
- Autovía (primary road) 120 km/h (75 mph)
- Carretera (A road) 90 km/h (56 mph)
- Built-up areas 40 km/h (25 mph)

the ticket on the windscreen. Parking in side streets is generally allowed except where the kerbstones are painted yellow (or green and white in bus-stop areas). Never park where you should not – yellow lines mean 'do not park here' – since they are very quick to tow you away. They have special vehicles called *gruas*, which take the car to a designated place, normally difficult to find, and of course you have to pay to get it back.

Useful words for drivers
- *aparcamiento* parking
- *estacionamiento prohibido* no parking
- *ceda el paso* give way to the right and left
- *circunvalación* ring road

Public transport
Current bus timetables are available from tourist offices. A regular and reliable bus service operates on the island. Like the spokes of a wheel, buses mostly operate directly into and out of the capital. This means a change of bus is often necessary to reach a particular destination. It pays to be on the early side since buses sometimes run marginally ahead of schedule. Not all services operate on Sunday. The Canarian word for bus, *guagua*, is pronounced 'wah-wah'. The main resorts are connected to the capital, with a frequent bus service, mostly half-hourly.

Air The local airline, **Binter Canarias**, provides regular flights between the islands. Booking centre ☎ 902 391 392 🌐 www.bintercanarias.com

Ferries and hydrofoils A complex network of inter-island ferries and hydrofoils links the seven main islands of the Canaries, and schedules change very regularly, so you need to check times locally. Inter-island services are operated by **Trasmediterranean** (🌐 www.trasmediterranea.es), **Naviera Armas** (☎ 902 456 500 🌐 www.naviera-armas.com) and the **Fred Olsen Express Line** (timetable details and online booking at 🌐 www.fredolsen.es).

Taxis Official taxis can be easily recognised by the sign on the roof. Next to the sign is a light that shows green when the taxi is free. Generally, short journeys within town are not expensive, especially with four people sharing. The taxis are colour coded according to the district in which they operate. For longer journeys you should agree a price in advance.

HEALTH, SAFETY & CRIME
Health
The sun is very strong at all times of the year so take great care with sunbathing, even when there is a cool breeze. Use high-factor creams initially and limit your sunbathing hours. Cover up at midday and in the early afternoon when the sun is at its highest. Remember, a slow tan is deeper and lasts longer. Do not let sunburn ruin your holiday!

Chemists Easily recognised by the big green cross above the door with the word *Farmacia*, chemists are very good on the islands, supplying everything you might need including antibiotics, which you can buy over the counter. The staff are always very helpful and knowledgeable – if you want something that they do not have in stock, they will normally get it for you very quickly.

Clinics All resorts have clinics where English is spoken. If you have minor ailments or injuries it is often better and faster to go to the Centro de Salud (the social security health centre), rather than to the hospital emergency department. All have fully qualified doctors and nursing staff and you can use your EHIC (see page 112).

Water Tap water is produced by desalination. It is not unsafe but does not taste good and is rich in minerals, which can cause upset stomachs. It is recommended that you drink bottled water.

Crime prevention
Take as much care of your personal property as you would at home. Watch out for pickpockets, especially in crowded marketplaces. Crime

with violence is unusual, but do not take risks. Leave nothing of value in a parked car, not even locked in the boot. Bag snatchers are around, too, so carry your valuables in a bag securely anchored to your body.

Lost property Report any loss or theft to your holiday representative. If an insurance claim is to be made, you must report thefts within 24 hours to the Municipal Police or Guardia Civil, from whom an official report must be obtained.

Police If you have a problem – say with lost or stolen property – talk to your holiday representative or hotel desk; they can help you make an official statement to the police. There are basically two types of police force on the island: La Policía Municipal, who come under the local authority at the Town Hall (Ayuntamiento), are responsible for law and

◯ *The island's beaches are particularly clean*

order in the local authority area and also traffic control. They wear dark blue uniforms. The other kind are La Guardia Civil (Civil Guard) and they are responsible for law and order in the rural areas, and traffic control on main roads and cities. If you commit an offence while driving, they are the ones that will stop and fine you. They wear green uniforms.

MEDIA

There is one English newspaper in Fuerteventura, *Fuertenews*, which is published in Corralejo. Local radio stations include Power FM which broadcasts across the Canaries between 91 and 92 MHz. QFM broadcasts on 98 MHz. These days, if you want serious news you can access the BBC World Service online. It's also possible, if you have access to some digital packages, to watch EuroNews, a pan-European magazine-style news programme. Coming from France – the adverts are in French – it broadcasts in different European languages simultaneously, and whether you can get the English version will depend on the settings on the digital receiver. British newspapers can be found easily in all the holiday resorts, although the price mark-ups can often be steep.

OPENING HOURS

Normal shopping hours are 09.00–13.00 and 17.00–20.00. Sunday is a general closing day. Shopping hours are not rigidly followed, especially in tourist areas. Supermarkets and bakeries often open earlier, usually by 08.30, and there are always some that stay open all day. Many shops relying on tourism stay open until late evening, closing at around 22.00.

RELIGION

Spain is a Catholic country, and Fuerteventura is no exception. You should bear in mind that in some places certain behaviour is inappropriate. You shouldn't wear a swimming costume to wander around a church, for example. If you want to attend Mass, services are usually on Saturday afternoon or Sunday morning. In smaller, more remote towns and villages the church is still very much at the heart of village life and it's only polite to respect this.

TIME DIFFERENCES

There is no time difference between the Canaries and the UK. The clocks go forward in March and back in October simultaneously.

TIPPING

As a tourist you would probably be expected to tip around 10 per cent. However, in less touristy places you'll notice that the Spanish often don't tip to a formula, but instead round up to the nearest euro or five euros, depending on the size of the bill and what coins and notes are being used. Don't feel under pressure, though – leave what you feel is deserved.

TOILETS

The days of finding a grubby pissoir out the back of a restaurant are generally over. Most bars and restaurants in Spain as a whole now have clean and modern bathrooms. However, except for some beaches, public toilets are generally non-existent.

TRAVELLERS WITH DISABILITIES

Spain's commitment to people with disabilities has been second to none over the last decade or two. You'll find that museums and other public buildings will often have facilities to cater for the needs of visitors with a disability. Spain's national association for the disabled, the Confederación Coordinadora Estatal de Minusválidos Físicos de España (COCEMFE), has a travel company, Servi-COCEMFE, based in Madrid, that provides information for travellers with a disability to Spain as a whole. ☎ 914 138 001 Ⓦ www.cocemfe.es (spanish only)

Europe For All An excellent new online information service for travellers with disabilities within Europe. Ⓦ www.europeforall.com

RADAR The principal UK forum and pressure group for people with disabilities. Ⓐ 12 City Forum, 250 City Road, London EC1V 8AF ☎ 020 7250 3222 Ⓦ www.radar.org.uk

SATH (Society for Accessible Travel & Hospitality) Advises US-based travellers with disabilities. Ⓐ 347 Fifth Ave, Suite 605, New York, NY 10016 ☎ 212 447 7284 Ⓦ www.sath.org

El Faro del Tostón on the northern coast